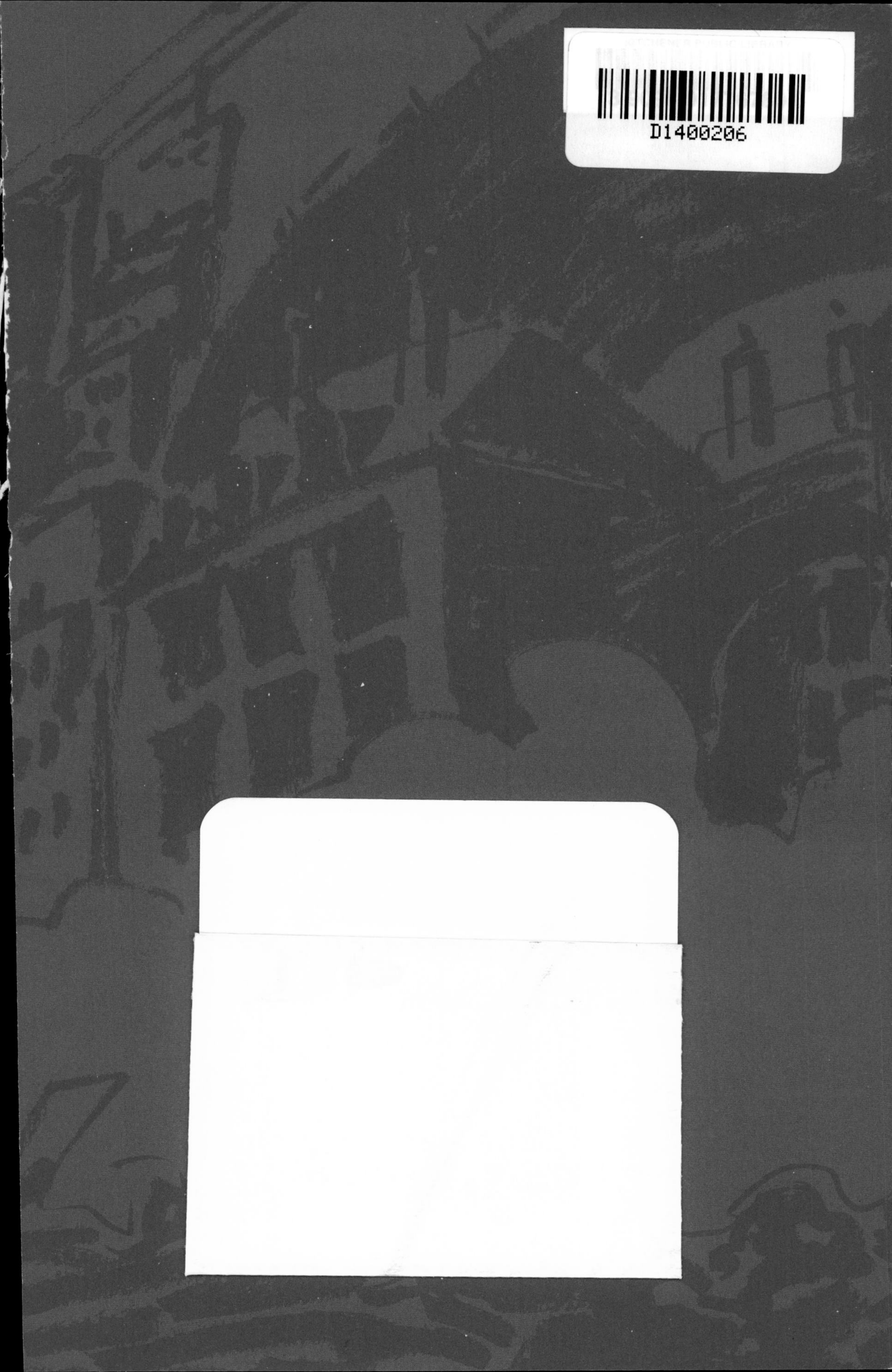

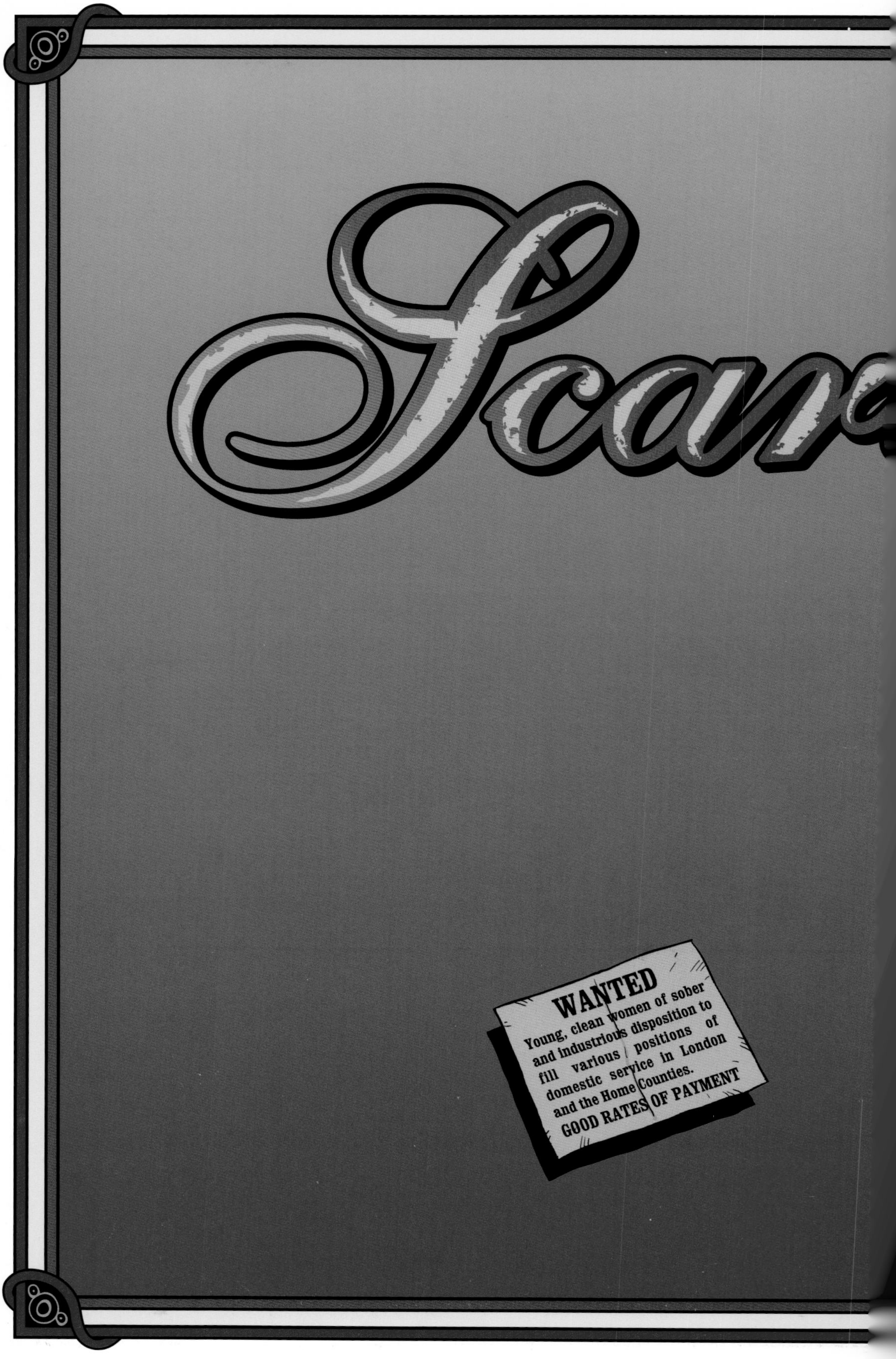
WANTED
Young, clean women of sober and industrious disposition to fill various positions of domestic service in London and the Home Counties.
GOOD RATES OF PAYMENT

let Traces ™

story
Ian Edginton

art
D'Israeli

Dark Horse Books™

publisher ~ Mike Richardson
art director ~ Mark Cox
designer ~ Amy Arendts
assistant editor ~ Philip W. Simon
editor ~ Dave Land

SCARLET TRACES™

Published by
Dark Horse Books
A division of Dark Horse Comics, Inc.
10956 SE Main Street
Milwaukie, OR 97222

www.darkhorse.com

To find a comics shop in your area call the Comic Shop Locator Service toll-free at (888) 266-4226

First edition: August 2003
ISBN-10: 1-56971-940-3
ISBN-13: 978-1-56971-940-4

10 9 8 7 6 5 4 3 2
Printed in China

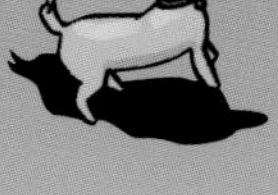

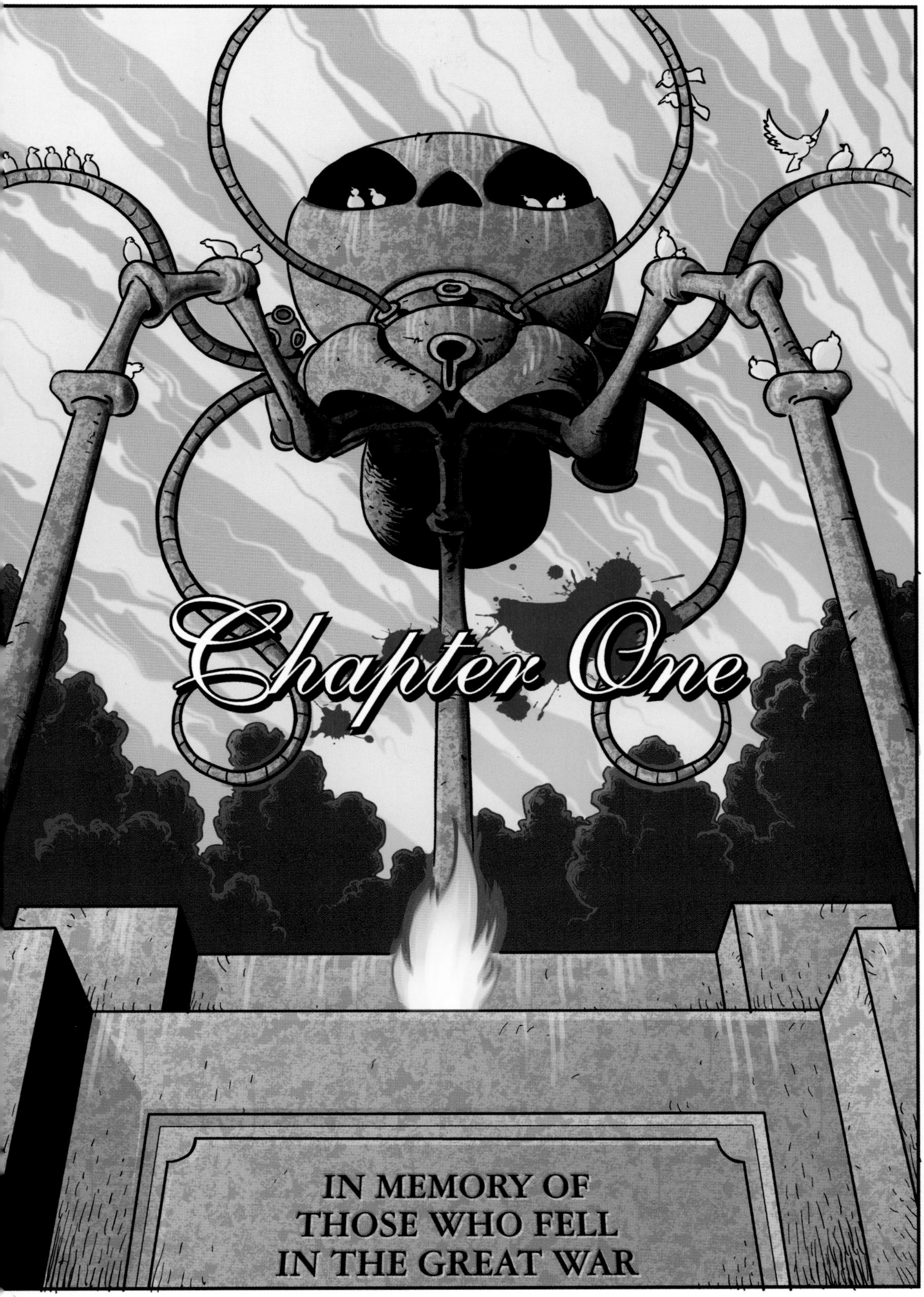
Chapter One
IN MEMORY OF
THOSE WHO FELL
IN THE GREAT WAR

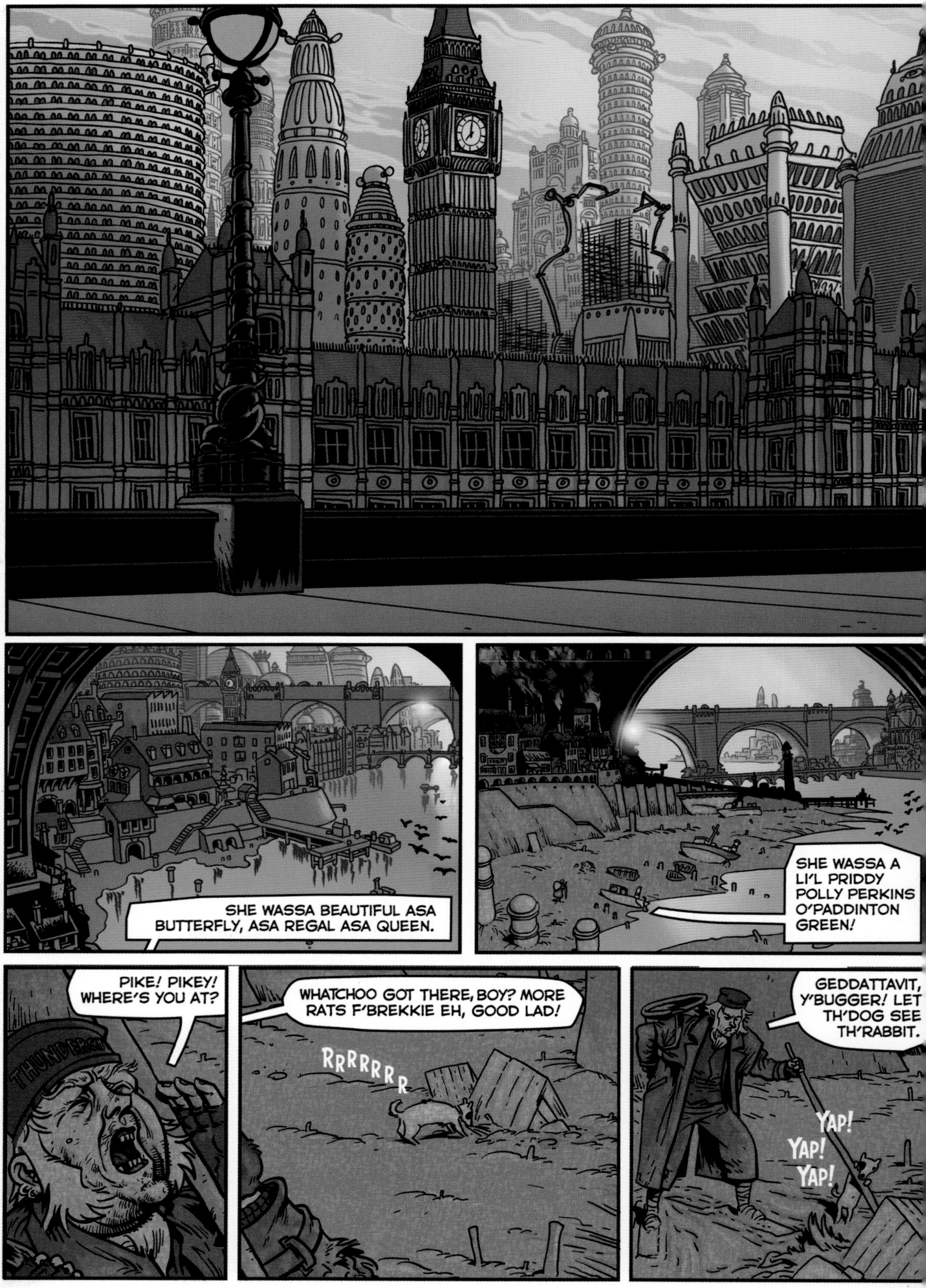
SHE WASSA BEAUTIFUL ASA BUTTERFLY, ASA REGAL ASA QUEEN.
SHE WASSA A LI'L PRIDDY POLLY PERKINS O'PADDINTON GREEN!
PIKE! PIKEY! WHERE'S YOU AT?
THUNDER
WHATCHOO GOT THERE, BOY? MORE RATS F'BREKKIE EH, GOOD LAD!
RRRRRRR
GEDDATTAVIT, Y'BUGGER! LET TH'DOG SEE TH'RABBIT.
YAP!
YAP!
YAP!

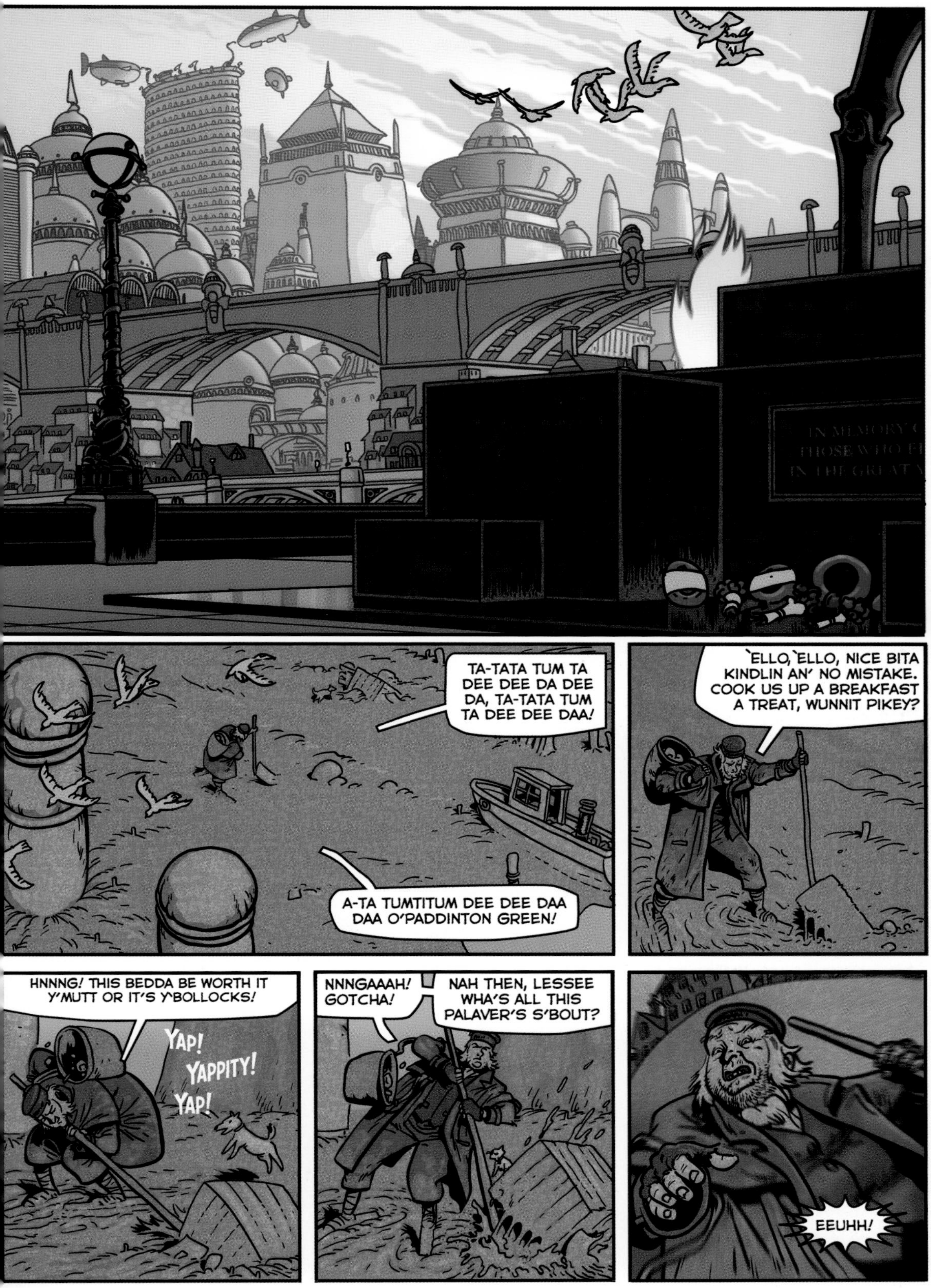
IN MEMORY
THOSE WHO
IN THE GREAT
TA-TATA TUM TA DEE DEE DA DEE DA, TA-TATA TUM TA DEE DEE DAA!
A-TA TUMTITUM DEE DEE DAA DAA O'PADDINTON GREEN!
`ELLO, `ELLO, NICE BITA KINDLIN AN' NO MISTAKE. COOK US UP A BREAKFAST A TREAT, WUNNIT PIKEY?
HNNNG! THIS BEDDA BE WORTH IT Y'MUTT OR IT'S Y'BOLLOCKS!
YAP!
YAPPITY!
YAP!
NNNGAAAH! GOTCHA!
NAH THEN, LESSEE WHA'S ALL THIS PALAVER'S S'BOUT?
EEUHH!

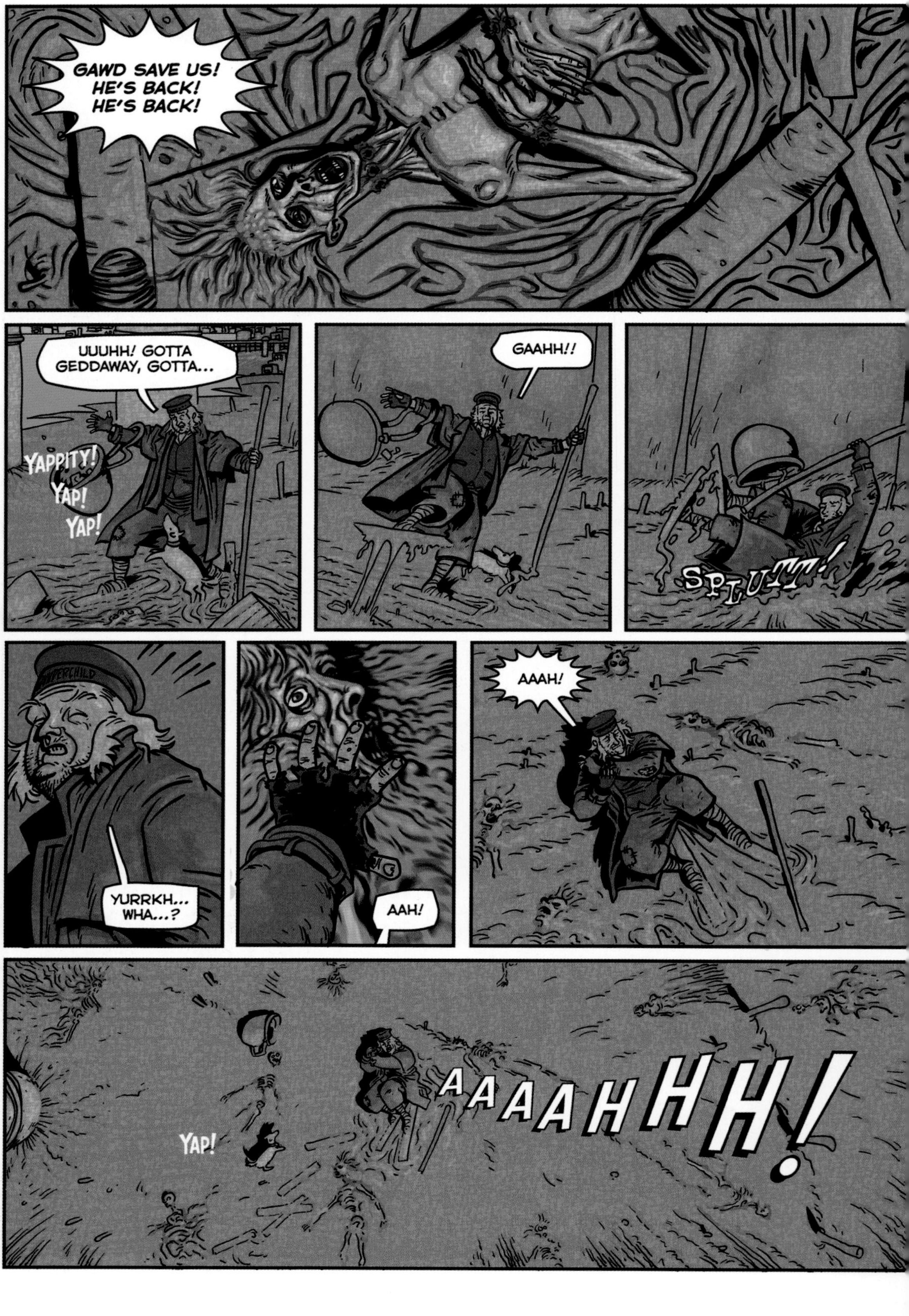
GAWD SAVE US! HE'S BACK! HE'S BACK!
UUUHH! GOTTA GEDDAWAY, GOTTA...
YAPPITY!
YAP!
YAP!
GAAHH!!
SPLUTT!
YURRKH... WHA...?
AAH!
AAAH!
AAAAHHHH!
YAP!

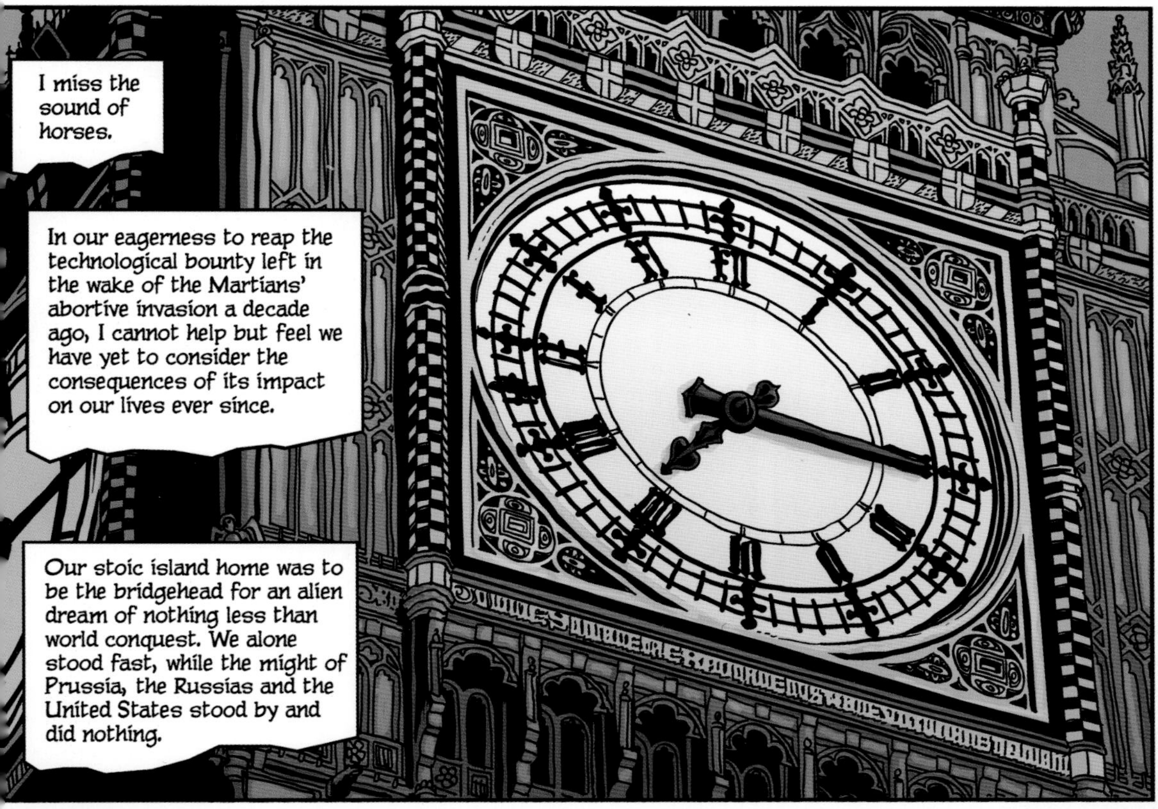
I miss the sound of horses.
In our eagerness to reap the technological bounty left in the wake of the Martians' abortive invasion a decade ago, I cannot help but feel we have yet to consider the consequences of its impact on our lives ever since.
Our stoic island home was to be the bridgehead for an alien dream of nothing less than world conquest. We alone stood fast, while the might of Prussia, the Russias and the United States stood by and did nothing.

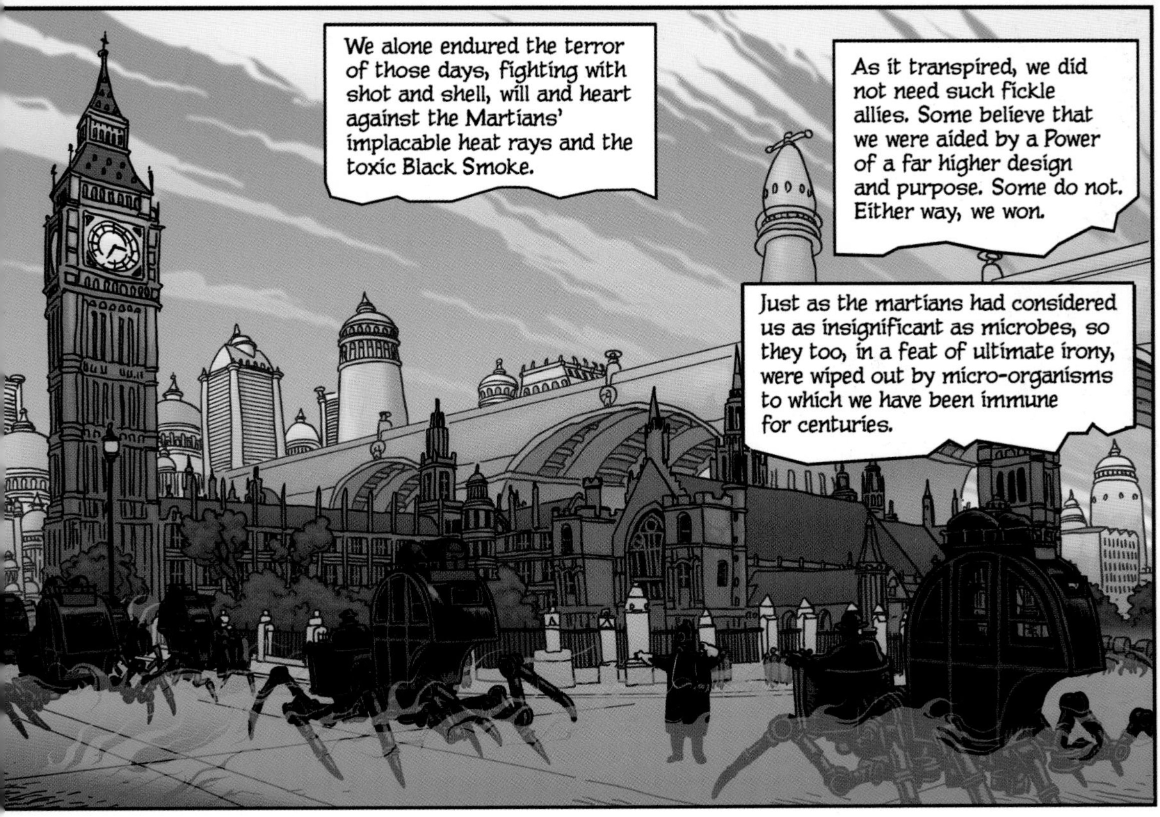
We alone endured the terror of those days, fighting with shot and shell, will and heart against the Martians' implacable heat rays and the toxic Black Smoke.
As it transpired, we did not need such fickle allies. Some believe that we were aided by a Power of a far higher design and purpose. Some do not. Either way, we won.
Just as the martians had considered us as insignificant as microbes, so they too, in a feat of ultimate irony, were wiped out by micro-organisms to which we have been immune for centuries.

The Martians' unwitting bequest to their would-be slaves was a form of technology as then undreamt of by mankind.

Within a decade our brightest minds had unravelled its secrets, their machineries of war and subjugation adapted and assimilated into our everyday usage.

The noble steed -- our companion and carriage for millennia is replaced by a clockwork toy! Homes are heated and lit by a version of the once-dreaded heat ray. The great mills and factories of the North are now vast, mechanised estates.

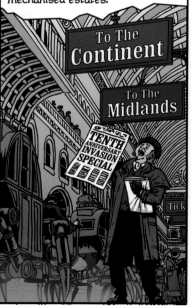

The British Empire is now truly a world power without peer, but I cannot help but wonder if we have not lost something in the process.

We have saved the world and become the envy of it... or rather feared by it.

All in all, we as a people have triumphed through adversity and attained an unexpected reward that benefits us all.

However, while the Martians were thwarted, we have in some insidious way succumbed to a form of conquest by proxy...

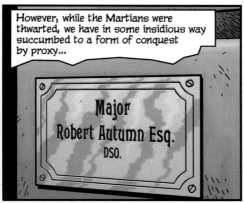

Major
Robert Autumn Esq.
DSO.

...and life, as we know it, will never be the same again.

edford quare

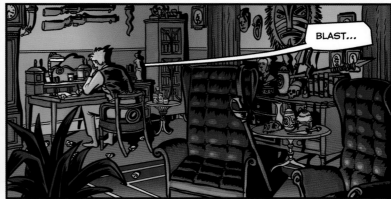

BLAST...

NOK NOK!

ENTER.

MORNIN' SIR!

AH, SERGEANT. IS IT REVEILLE ALREADY?

AYE. DID YE NO AWAY T'YE BED AGAIN LAST NIGHT?

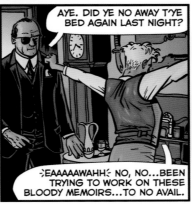

⸝EAAAAAWAHH⸝ NO, NO...BEEN TRYING TO WORK ON THESE BLOODY MEMOIRS...TO NO AVAIL.

THAT'S NO ALL Y'BEEN WORKIN' ON, EH?

QUITE. I THOUGHT IT MIGHT AID IN STIMULATING THE CREATIVE JUICES AND INSTEAD ENDED UP STEWING IN THEM.

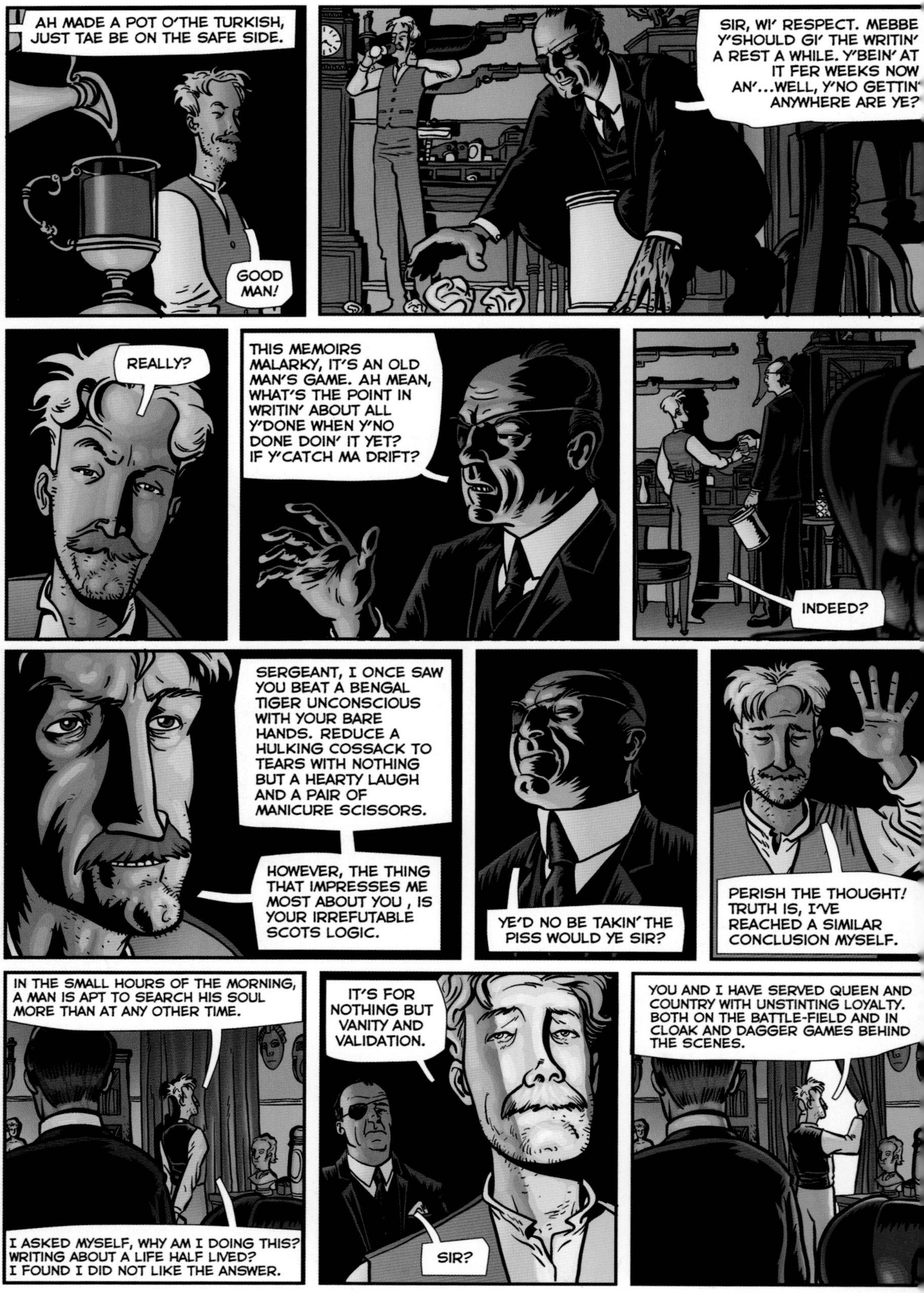
AH MADE A POT O'THE TURKISH, JUST TAE BE ON THE SAFE SIDE.
GOOD MAN!
SIR, WI' RESPECT. MEBBE Y'SHOULD GI' THE WRITIN' A REST A WHILE. Y'BEIN' AT IT FER WEEKS NOW AN'...WELL, Y'NO GETTIN' ANYWHERE ARE YE?
REALLY?
THIS MEMOIRS MALARKY, IT'S AN OLD MAN'S GAME. AH MEAN, WHAT'S THE POINT IN WRITIN' ABOUT ALL Y'DONE WHEN Y'NO DONE DOIN' IT YET? IF Y'CATCH MA DRIFT?
INDEED?
SERGEANT, I ONCE SAW YOU BEAT A BENGAL TIGER UNCONSCIOUS WITH YOUR BARE HANDS. REDUCE A HULKING COSSACK TO TEARS WITH NOTHING BUT A HEARTY LAUGH AND A PAIR OF MANICURE SCISSORS.
HOWEVER, THE THING THAT IMPRESSES ME MOST ABOUT YOU , IS YOUR IRREFUTABLE SCOTS LOGIC.
YE'D NO BE TAKIN' THE PISS WOULD YE SIR?
PERISH THE THOUGHT! TRUTH IS, I'VE REACHED A SIMILAR CONCLUSION MYSELF.
IN THE SMALL HOURS OF THE MORNING, A MAN IS APT TO SEARCH HIS SOUL MORE THAN AT ANY OTHER TIME.
I ASKED MYSELF, WHY AM I DOING THIS? WRITING ABOUT A LIFE HALF LIVED? I FOUND I DID NOT LIKE THE ANSWER.
IT'S FOR NOTHING BUT VANITY AND VALIDATION.
SIR?
YOU AND I HAVE SERVED QUEEN AND COUNTRY WITH UNSTINTING LOYALTY. BOTH ON THE BATTLE-FIELD AND IN CLOAK AND DAGGER GAMES BEHIND THE SCENES.

YET IN RECENT YEARS IT FEELS AS IF WE HAVE BEEN PUT OUT TO PASTURE.

WE HAVE BEEN ECLIPSED BY THE TIMES, OLD FRIEND. THE FUTURE HAS OVERTAKEN US AND LEFT US STANDING IN ITS DUST.

WHO WANTS TO READ ABOUT A SOLDIER'S LIFE, WHEN THEY HAVE ALL THIS ON THEIR DOORSTEP?

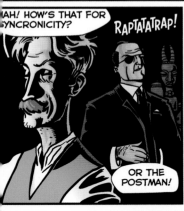

AH! HOW'S THAT FOR SYNCRONICITY?

RAPTATATRAP!

OR THE POSTMAN!

RAPTATATRAP!

AWRIGHT! AWRIGHT! KEEP Y'BREEKS ON!

GOOD MORNIN' GENTLEMEN. HOW MAY I...

ARCHIBALD SOLOMON CURRIE?

AYE. CAN AH HELP YOU?

THAT'S FOR ME TO DECIDE, SONNY JIM.

IS THAT RIGHT? AN' WHO MIGHT YOU BE PALLY?

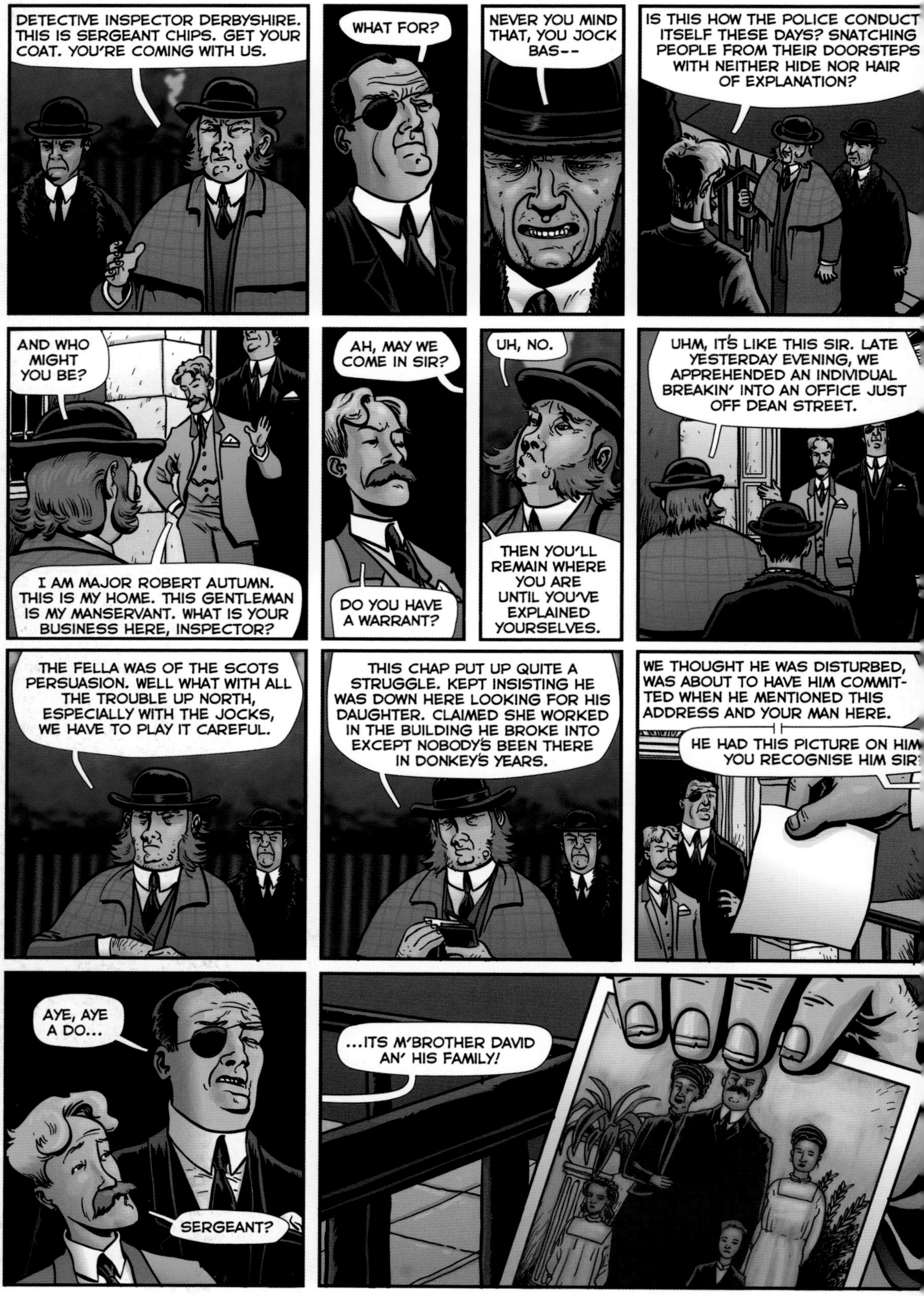
DETECTIVE INSPECTOR DERBYSHIRE. THIS IS SERGEANT CHIPS. GET YOUR COAT. YOU'RE COMING WITH US.
WHAT FOR?
NEVER YOU MIND THAT, YOU JOCK BAS--
IS THIS HOW THE POLICE CONDUCT ITSELF THESE DAYS? SNATCHING PEOPLE FROM THEIR DOORSTEPS WITH NEITHER HIDE NOR HAIR OF EXPLANATION?
AND WHO MIGHT YOU BE?
I AM MAJOR ROBERT AUTUMN. THIS IS MY HOME. THIS GENTLEMAN IS MY MANSERVANT. WHAT IS YOUR BUSINESS HERE, INSPECTOR?
AH, MAY WE COME IN SIR?
DO YOU HAVE A WARRANT?
UH, NO.
THEN YOU'LL REMAIN WHERE YOU ARE UNTIL YOU'VE EXPLAINED YOURSELVES.
UHM, IT'S LIKE THIS SIR. LATE YESTERDAY EVENING, WE APPREHENDED AN INDIVIDUAL BREAKIN' INTO AN OFFICE JUST OFF DEAN STREET.
THE FELLA WAS OF THE SCOTS PERSUASION. WELL WHAT WITH ALL THE TROUBLE UP NORTH, ESPECIALLY WITH THE JOCKS, WE HAVE TO PLAY IT CAREFUL.
THIS CHAP PUT UP QUITE A STRUGGLE. KEPT INSISTING HE WAS DOWN HERE LOOKING FOR HIS DAUGHTER. CLAIMED SHE WORKED IN THE BUILDING HE BROKE INTO EXCEPT NOBODY'S BEEN THERE IN DONKEY'S YEARS.
WE THOUGHT HE WAS DISTURBED, WAS ABOUT TO HAVE HIM COMMITTED WHEN HE MENTIONED THIS ADDRESS AND YOUR MAN HERE.
HE HAD THIS PICTURE ON HIM YOU RECOGNISE HIM SIR?
AYE, AYE A DO...
SERGEANT?
...ITS M'BROTHER DAVID AN' HIS FAMILY!

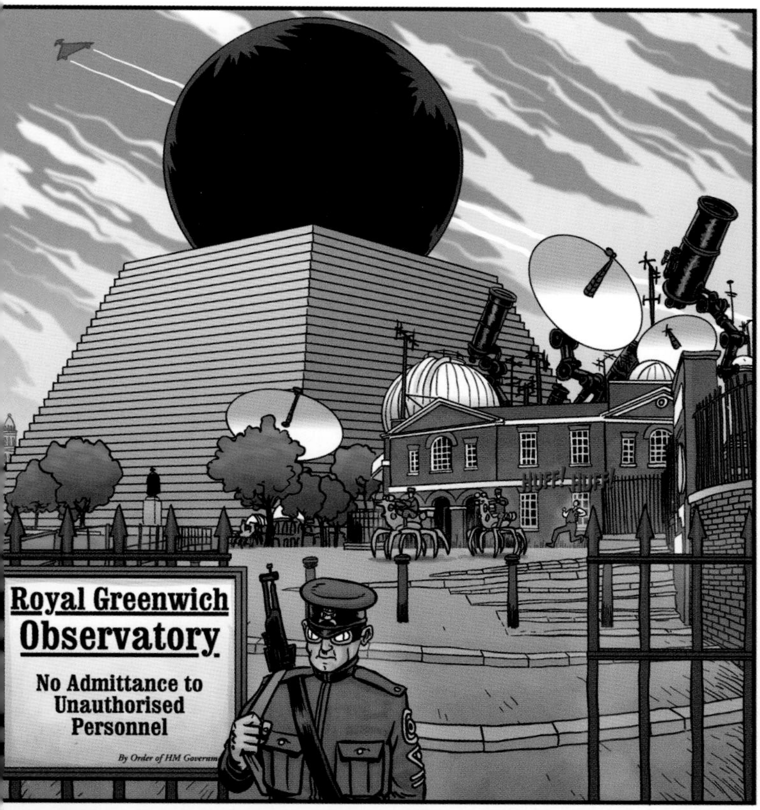
Royal Greenwich
Observatory
No Admittance to
Unauthorised
Personnel
HUFF! HUFF!

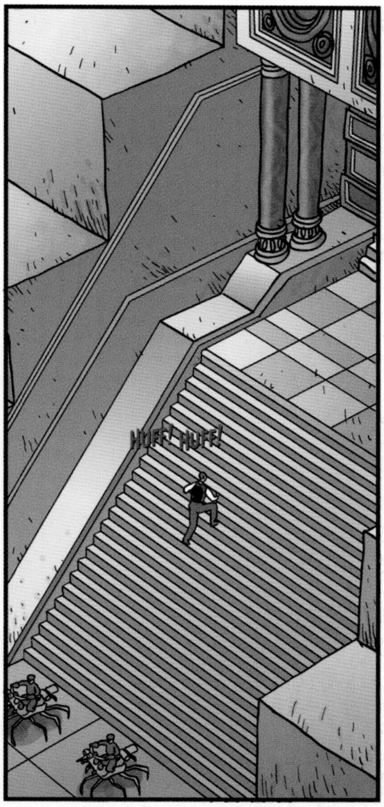
HUFF! HUFF!

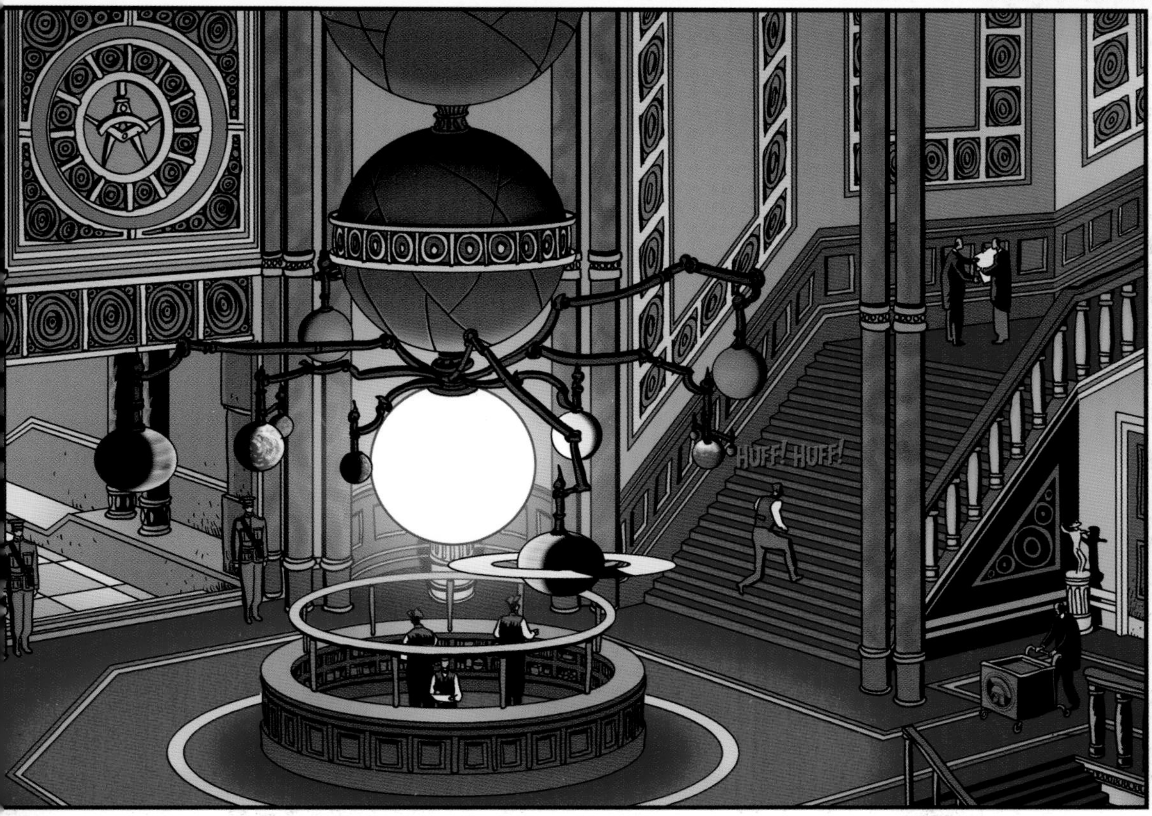
HUFF! HUFF!

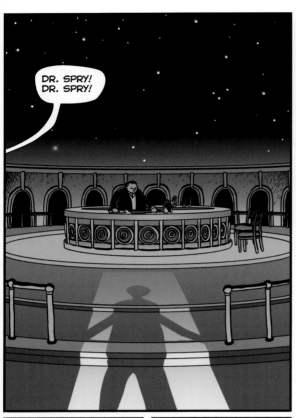

SHE'S JUST GONE, AWRIGHT! SHE'S DEAD! DISAPPEARED! GONE!! GEDDIT!

AW CHRIST ALMIGHTY ARCH'. AH'M SORRY. SHE'S MA WEE GIRL. AH...AH DUNNO WHUT TAE DO ANY MORE...

AH KNOW. I'M HERE TAE HELP. TELL ME, WHAT WAS SHE DOIN' ALL ALONE IN LONDON?

ARCHIE MAN, WHERE'VE YE BEEN? D'YE NOT KNOW HOW IT IS BACK HOME?

THERE'S NAE WORK...NOTHIN'. IT'S TH' MACHINES. THE MILLS AN' SHIPYARDS ARE ALL AUTOMATED. A HUNDRED MEN DO THE WORK O'A THOUSAND.

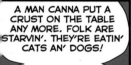

A MAN CANNA PUT A CRUST ON THE TABLE ANY MORE. FOLK ARE STARVIN'. THEY'RE EATIN' CATS AN' DOGS!

AN' THE WOMEN, THERE'S NOTHIN' F'THEM BUT WHORIN'. THERE'S BAIRNS OF TEN AN' TWELVE WORKIN' TH'CORNERS FER HA'PENNIES.

KATIE?

NAW, GOD BLESS HER. SHE FOUND WORK WI' SOME AGENCY THAT CAME LOOKIN' FER GIRLS TAE GO INTO SERVICE DOWN SOUTH, MAIDS AN' TH' LIKE.

SHE WROTE EVERY COUPLE O' DAYS, SENT MONEY WHEN SHE COULD. IT WAS ALL FINE FER A COUPLE O' WEEKS, THEN NOTHIN'. NOT A WORD.

DAVY, WHY DIDN'T Y'CONTACT ME?

HOW? WHAT WITH? EVEN WI' KATIE'S MONEY WE WAS JUST SCRAPIN' BY. I HADDA JUMP A FREIGHT TRAIN T'GET HERE M'SEL'!

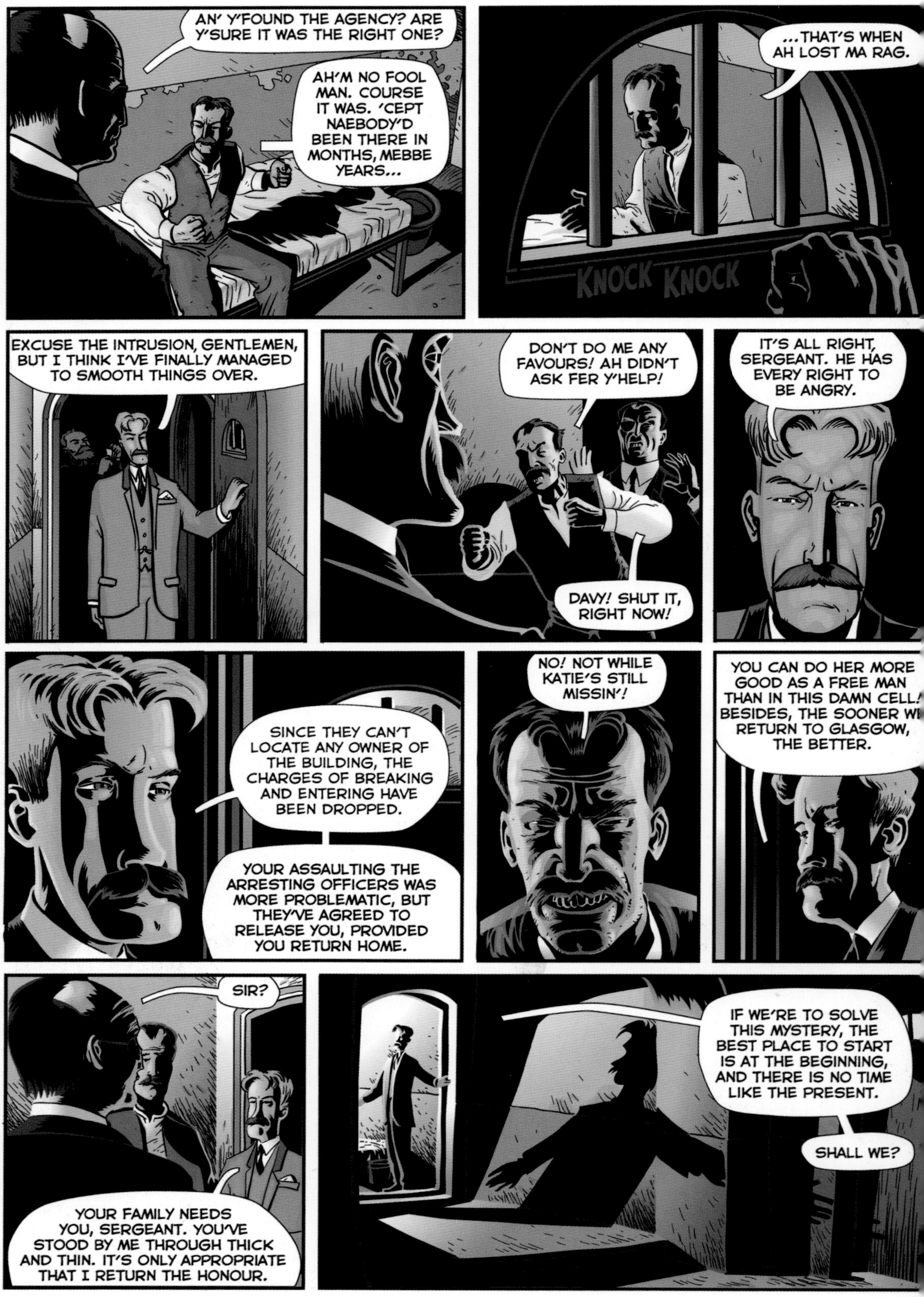
AN' Y'FOUND THE AGENCY? ARE Y'SURE IT WAS THE RIGHT ONE?
AH'M NO FOOL MAN. COURSE IT WAS. 'CEPT NAEBODY'D BEEN THERE IN MONTHS, MEBBE YEARS...
...THAT'S WHEN AH LOST MA RAG.
KNOCK KNOCK
EXCUSE THE INTRUSION, GENTLEMEN, BUT I THINK I'VE FINALLY MANAGED TO SMOOTH THINGS OVER.
DON'T DO ME ANY FAVOURS! AH DIDN'T ASK FER Y'HELP!
DAVY! SHUT IT, RIGHT NOW!
IT'S ALL RIGHT, SERGEANT. HE HAS EVERY RIGHT TO BE ANGRY.
SINCE THEY CAN'T LOCATE ANY OWNER OF THE BUILDING, THE CHARGES OF BREAKING AND ENTERING HAVE BEEN DROPPED.
YOUR ASSAULTING THE ARRESTING OFFICERS WAS MORE PROBLEMATIC, BUT THEY'VE AGREED TO RELEASE YOU, PROVIDED YOU RETURN HOME.
NO! NOT WHILE KATIE'S STILL MISSIN'!
YOU CAN DO HER MORE GOOD AS A FREE MAN THAN IN THIS DAMN CELL! BESIDES, THE SOONER WE RETURN TO GLASGOW, THE BETTER.
SIR?
YOUR FAMILY NEEDS YOU, SERGEANT. YOU'VE STOOD BY ME THROUGH THICK AND THIN. IT'S ONLY APPROPRIATE THAT I RETURN THE HONOUR.
IF WE'RE TO SOLVE THIS MYSTERY, THE BEST PLACE TO START IS AT THE BEGINNING, AND THERE IS NO TIME LIKE THE PRESENT.
SHALL WE?

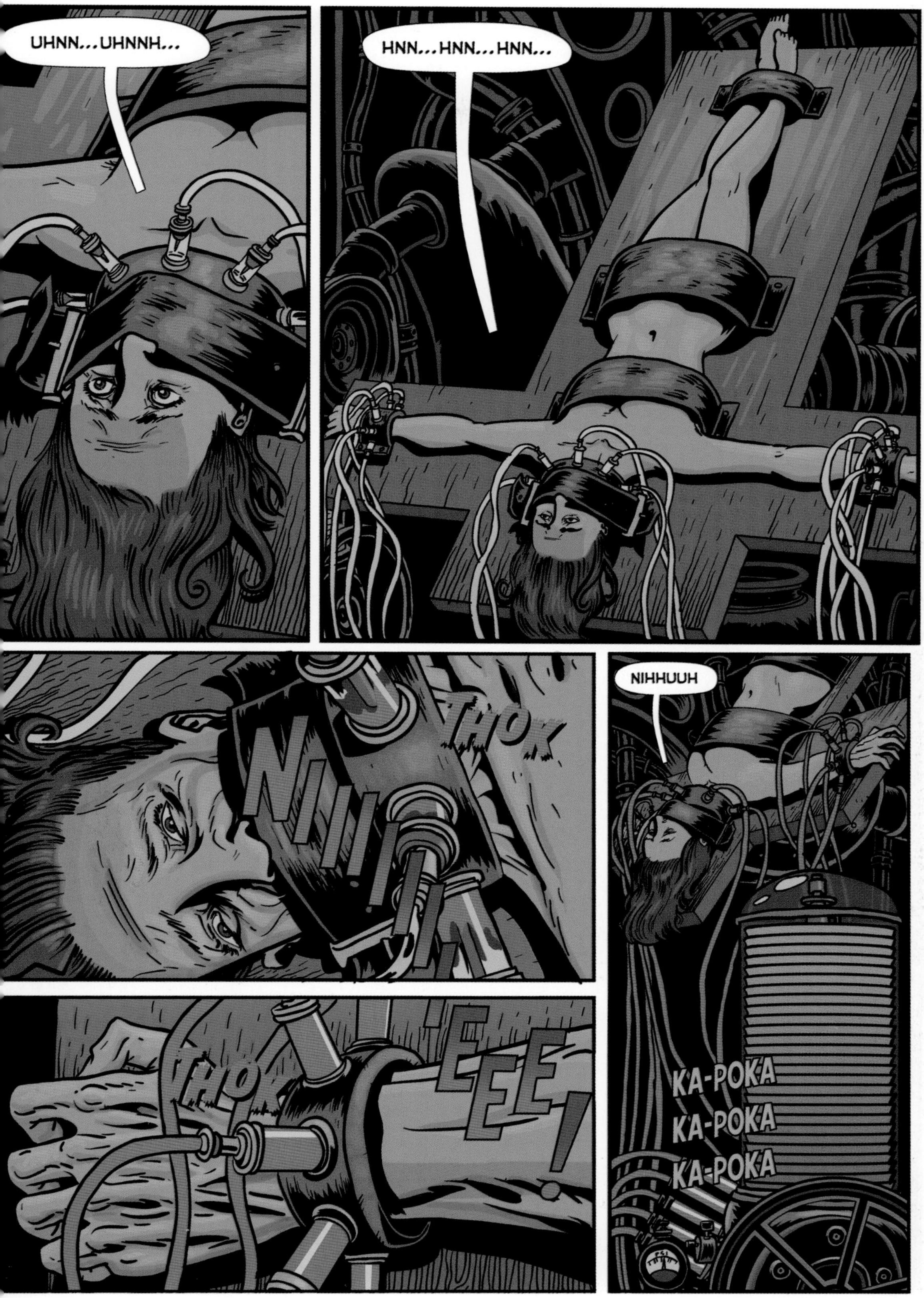
UHNN...UHNNH...
HNN...HNN...HNN...
THOK
NIHHUUH
KA-POKA
KA-POKA
KA-POKA
THOK

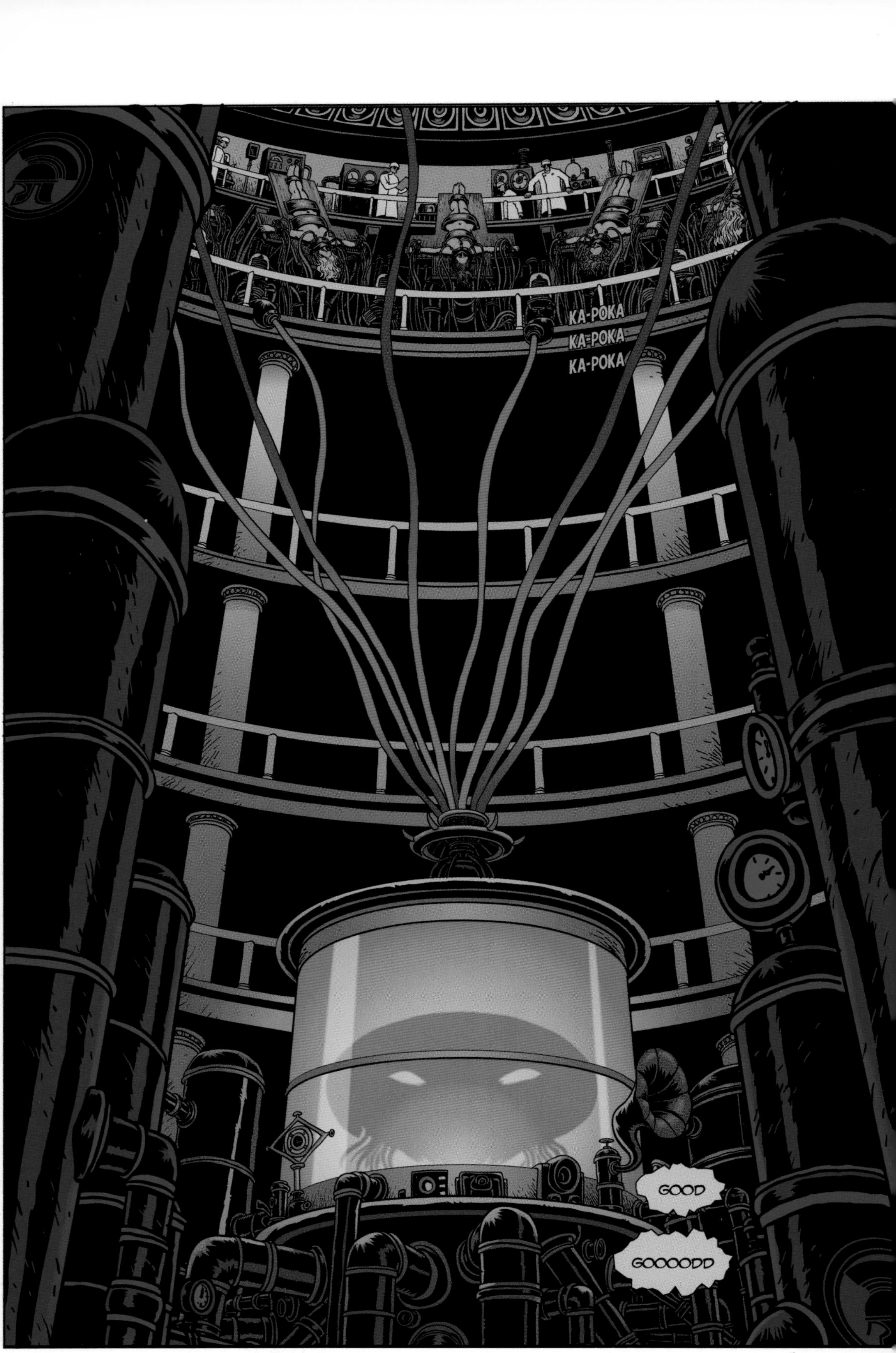
KA-POKA
KA-POKA
KA-POKA
GOOD
GOOOODD

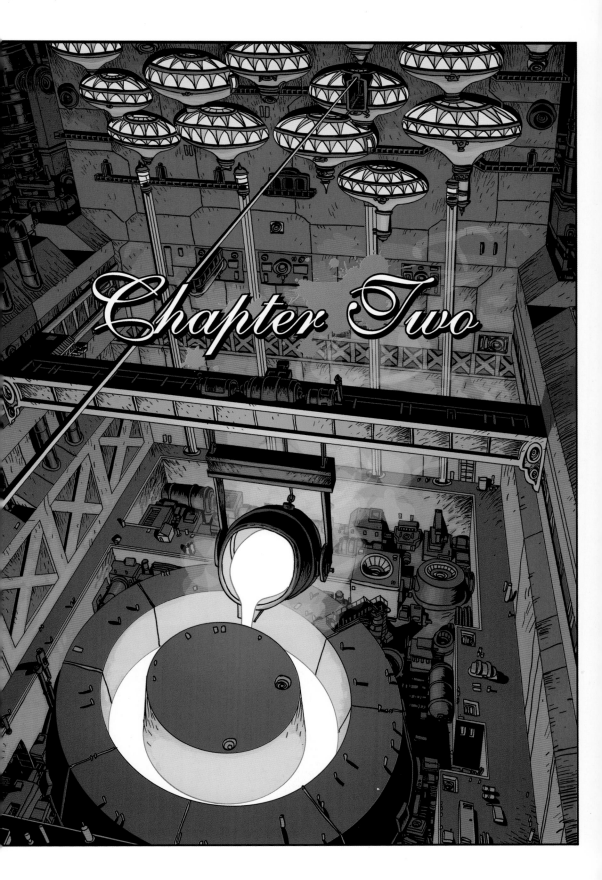

Chapter Two

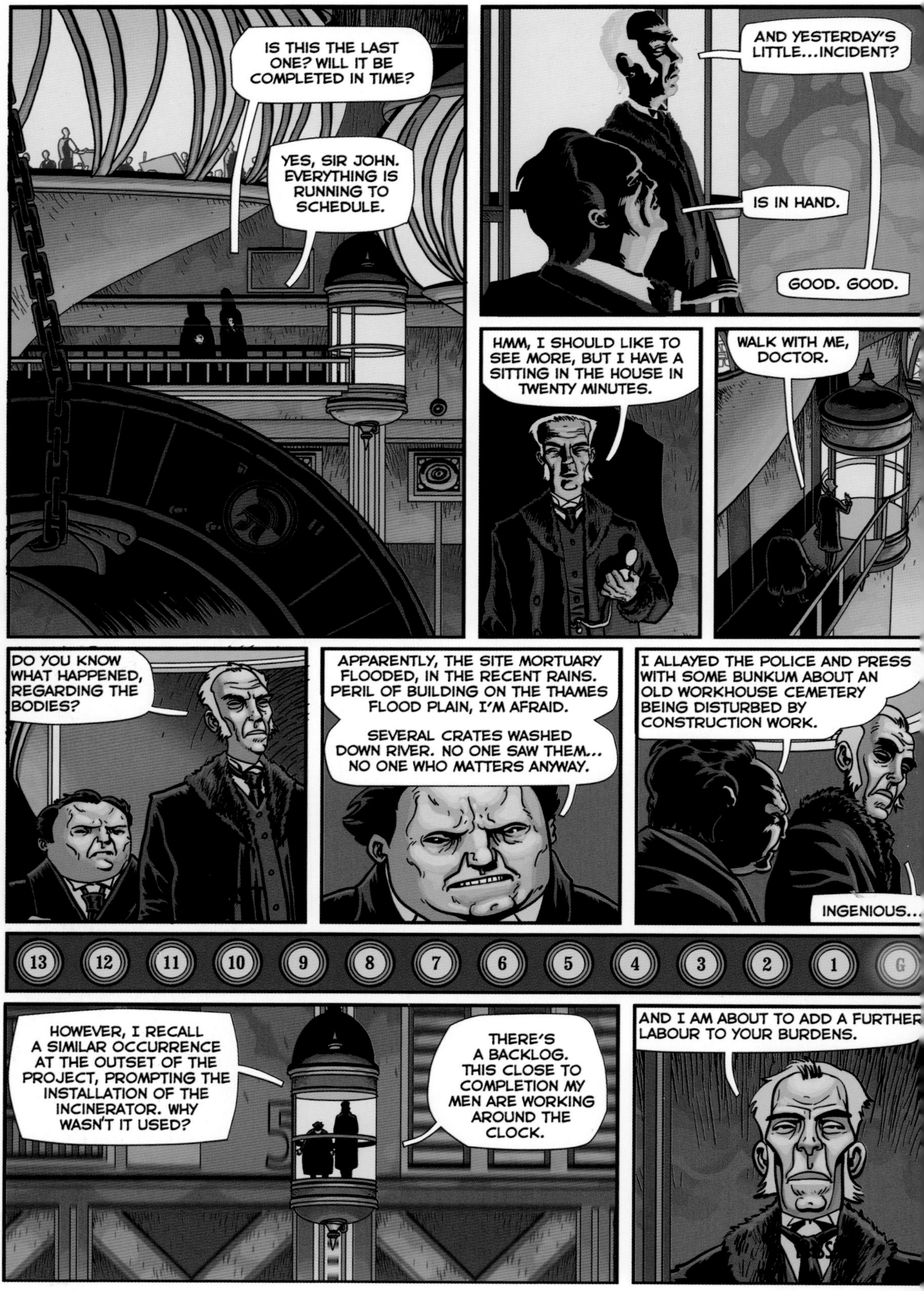
IS THIS THE LAST ONE? WILL IT BE COMPLETED IN TIME?
YES, SIR JOHN. EVERYTHING IS RUNNING TO SCHEDULE.
AND YESTERDAY'S LITTLE...INCIDENT?
IS IN HAND.
GOOD. GOOD.
HMM, I SHOULD LIKE TO SEE MORE, BUT I HAVE A SITTING IN THE HOUSE IN TWENTY MINUTES.
WALK WITH ME, DOCTOR.
DO YOU KNOW WHAT HAPPENED, REGARDING THE BODIES?
APPARENTLY, THE SITE MORTUARY FLOODED, IN THE RECENT RAINS. PERIL OF BUILDING ON THE THAMES FLOOD PLAIN, I'M AFRAID.
SEVERAL CRATES WASHED DOWN RIVER. NO ONE SAW THEM... NO ONE WHO MATTERS ANYWAY.
I ALLAYED THE POLICE AND PRESS WITH SOME BUNKUM ABOUT AN OLD WORKHOUSE CEMETERY BEING DISTURBED BY CONSTRUCTION WORK.
INGENIOUS...
13 12 11 10 9 8 7 6 5 4 3 2 1 G
HOWEVER, I RECALL A SIMILAR OCCURRENCE AT THE OUTSET OF THE PROJECT, PROMPTING THE INSTALLATION OF THE INCINERATOR. WHY WASN'T IT USED?
THERE'S A BACKLOG. THIS CLOSE TO COMPLETION MY MEN ARE WORKING AROUND THE CLOCK.
AND I AM ABOUT TO ADD A FURTHER LABOUR TO YOUR BURDENS.

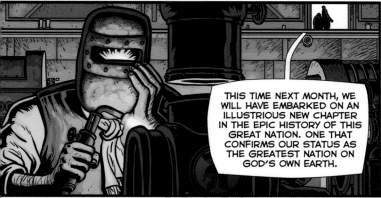

THIS TIME NEXT MONTH, WE WILL HAVE EMBARKED ON AN ILLUSTRIOUS NEW CHAPTER IN THE EPIC HISTORY OF THIS GREAT NATION. ONE THAT CONFIRMS OUR STATUS AS THE GREATEST NATION ON GOD'S OWN EARTH.

AND AS YOU KNOW, GOD IS AN ENGLISHMAN.

NOTHING MUST COMPROMISE THIS GOAL DOCTOR, NOTHING.

WE HAVE DONE MANY QUESTIONABLE THINGS TO REACH THIS POINT. NOW WE MUST GRIT OUR TEETH, GIRD OUR LOINS AND PUSH ON THAT EXTRA MILE. WE MUST WIPE THE SLATE CLEAN, DO YOU UNDERSTAND?

COMPLETELY.

DO YOU HAVE THE KIND OF MEN WHO ARE UP TO THE TASK?

INDEED I DO, SIR...

"...IN FACT I HAVE JUST THE PAIR IN MIND."

HOW IS HE SERGEANT?

STILL SLEEPIN' LIKE A BAIRN. WAS THE SUPPER THAT DID FER HIM. HE'S NO HAD A DECENT MEAL IN MONTHS.

WHISKY?

AYE.

I CONFESS, I HAD HEARD THINGS WERE GRIM IN THE NORTH, BUT FROM WHAT DAVID DESCRIBED, THEY ARE NOTHING SHORT OF HELLISH.

AN' THERE'S ME SITTIN' ON MA ARSE IN LONDON, IN THE LAP O'BLOODY LUXURY WHILE MA KIN GO HUNGRY.

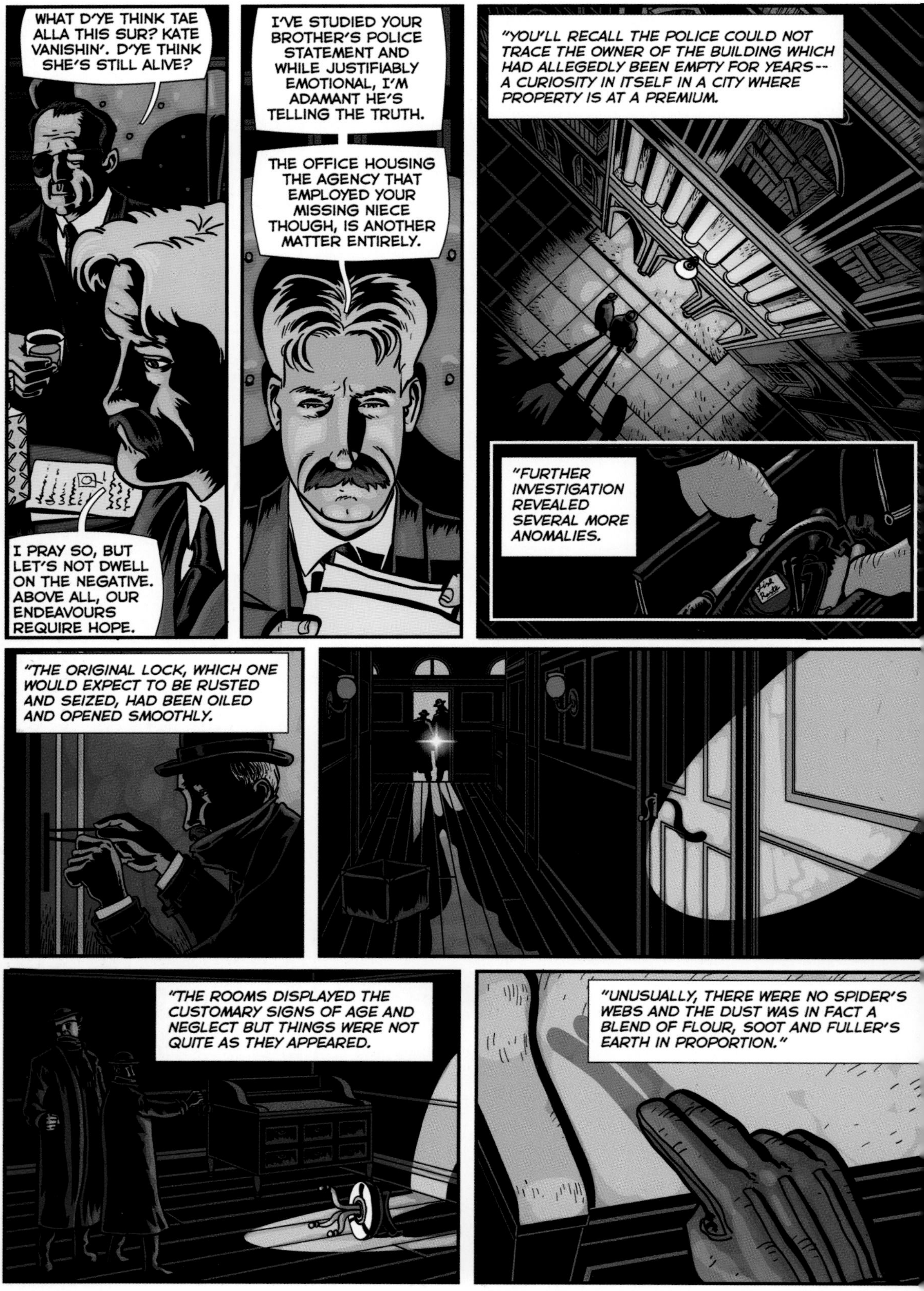
WHAT D'YE THINK TAE ALLA THIS SUR? KATE VANISHIN'. D'YE THINK SHE'S STILL ALIVE?
I PRAY SO, BUT LET'S NOT DWELL ON THE NEGATIVE. ABOVE ALL, OUR ENDEAVOURS REQUIRE HOPE.
I'VE STUDIED YOUR BROTHER'S POLICE STATEMENT AND WHILE JUSTIFIABLY EMOTIONAL, I'M ADAMANT HE'S TELLING THE TRUTH.
THE OFFICE HOUSING THE AGENCY THAT EMPLOYED YOUR MISSING NIECE THOUGH, IS ANOTHER MATTER ENTIRELY.
"YOU'LL RECALL THE POLICE COULD NOT TRACE THE OWNER OF THE BUILDING WHICH HAD ALLEGEDLY BEEN EMPTY FOR YEARS-- A CURIOSITY IN ITSELF IN A CITY WHERE PROPERTY IS AT A PREMIUM.
"FURTHER INVESTIGATION REVEALED SEVERAL MORE ANOMALIES.
"THE ORIGINAL LOCK, WHICH ONE WOULD EXPECT TO BE RUSTED AND SEIZED, HAD BEEN OILED AND OPENED SMOOTHLY.
"THE ROOMS DISPLAYED THE CUSTOMARY SIGNS OF AGE AND NEGLECT BUT THINGS WERE NOT QUITE AS THEY APPEARED.
"UNUSUALLY, THERE WERE NO SPIDER'S WEBS AND THE DUST WAS IN FACT A BLEND OF FLOUR, SOOT AND FULLER'S EARTH IN PROPORTION."

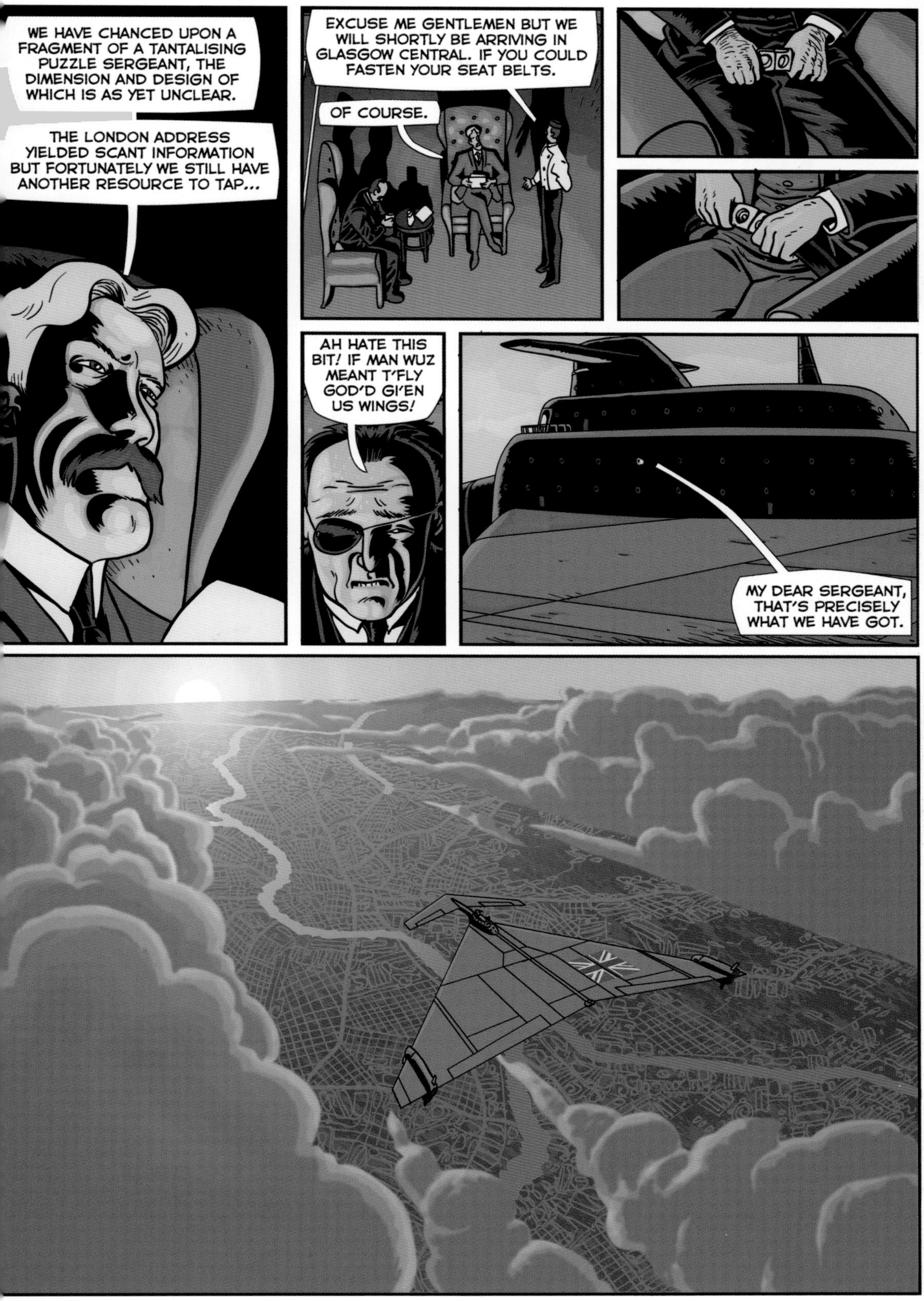
WE HAVE CHANCED UPON A FRAGMENT OF A TANTALISING PUZZLE SERGEANT, THE DIMENSION AND DESIGN OF WHICH IS AS YET UNCLEAR.
THE LONDON ADDRESS YIELDED SCANT INFORMATION BUT FORTUNATELY WE STILL HAVE ANOTHER RESOURCE TO TAP...
EXCUSE ME GENTLEMEN BUT WE WILL SHORTLY BE ARRIVING IN GLASGOW CENTRAL. IF YOU COULD FASTEN YOUR SEAT BELTS.
OF COURSE.
AH HATE THIS BIT! IF MAN WUZ MEANT T'FLY GOD'D GI'EN US WINGS!
MY DEAR SERGEANT, THAT'S PRECISELY WHAT WE HAVE GOT.

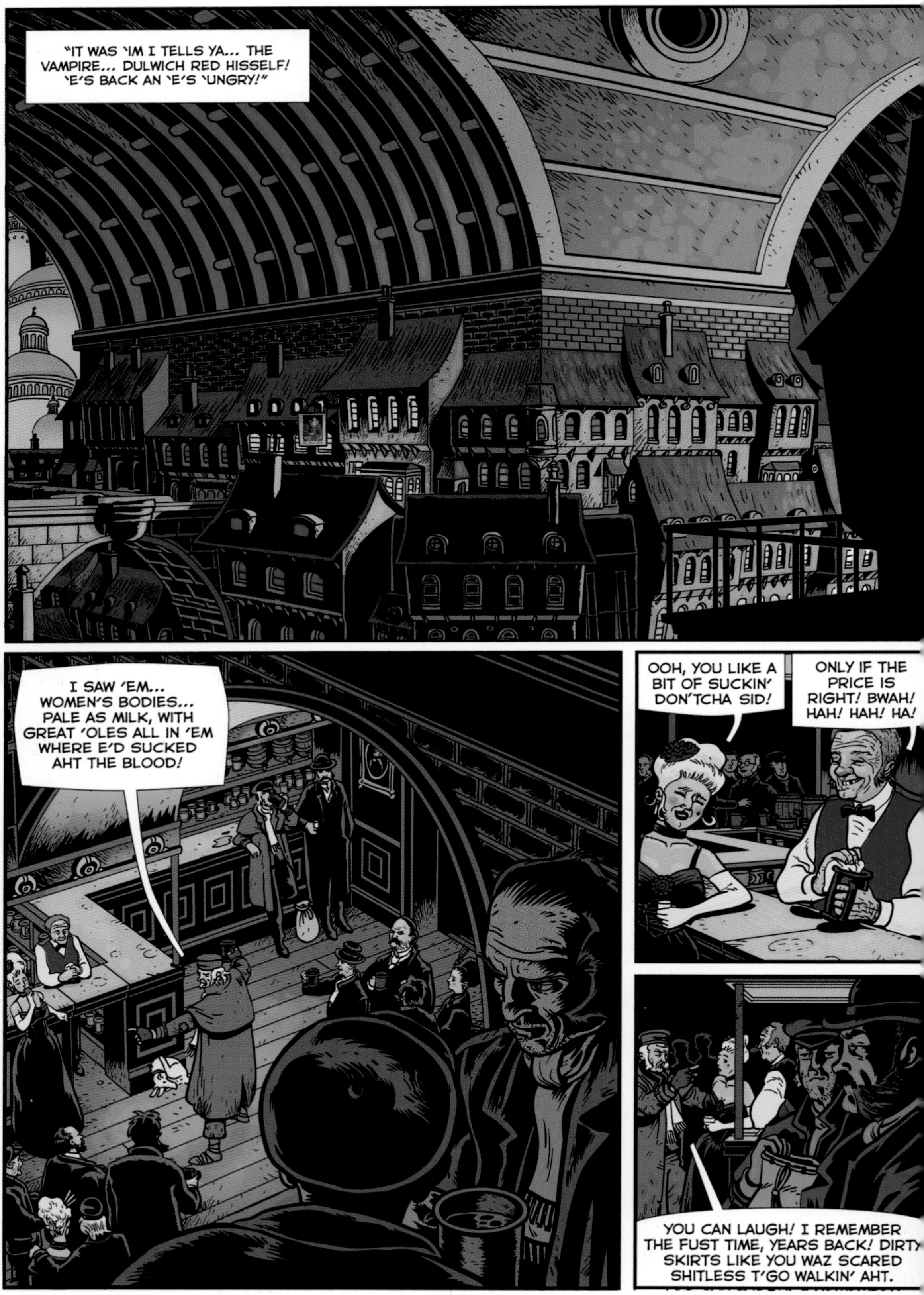
"IT WAS 'IM I TELLS YA... THE VAMPIRE... DULWICH RED HISSELF! 'E'S BACK AN 'E'S 'UNGRY!"
I SAW 'EM... WOMEN'S BODIES... PALE AS MILK, WITH GREAT 'OLES ALL IN 'EM WHERE E'D SUCKED AHT THE BLOOD!
OOH, YOU LIKE A BIT OF SUCKIN' DON'TCHA SID!
ONLY IF THE PRICE IS RIGHT! BWAH! HAH! HAH! HA!
YOU CAN LAUGH! I REMEMBER THE FUST TIME, YEARS BACK! DIRTY SKIRTS LIKE YOU WAZ SCARED SHITLESS T'GO WALKIN' AHT.

THERE'LL BE ANOTHER'UN IN A MINUTE IF Y'DON'T PACK IT IN, YOU OLD SOAK. Y'PUTTIN THE WIND UP THE PUNTERS.

YEAH, WE GOT A LIVIN' TO EARN 'ENT WE.

THERE WAS DEAD UN'S FLOATIN' ALL DAHN THE RIVER! 'US' LIKE THEM YESTERDAY!

AHH, Y'ALL BASTARDS AN' 'OOERS THE LOT O'YEH!

RIGHT, THAT'S IT! I'VE 'AD ENOUGH O'YOU Y'OLD FART!

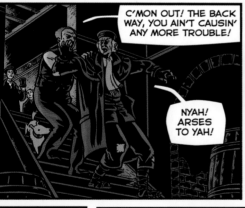

C'MON OUT! THE BACK WAY, YOU AIN'T CAUSIN' ANY MORE TROUBLE!

NYAH! ARSES TO YAH!

AN' TAKE Y'BLEEDIN' RAT WITH YOU AS WELL!

'RIKE!

EEY-YAHH!

27

SMASHIN'.

AYE.

PITY 'BOUT HIS DOG THOUGH. I WAS ALWAYS PARTIAL TO JACK RUSSELLS.

OH, NOT WALES? I HATE THEM SHEEP SHAGGERS!

HA! HA! HA! SAYS SOMETHIN' DON' IT WHEN THE PRETTIEST GALS THERE ARE THE ONES WIV FOUR LEGS.

WE AIN'T GOIN' THERE, DANNY BOY. DON'T WORRY.

WHERE TO NEXT PEACHY?

A GAFF IN DEAN STREET, THEN WE GOT AN EXPRESS FLIGHT TO CATCH. WE'RE OFF UP COUNTRY, TO THE WILDS.

SO WHERE ARE WE OFF TO?

LAND OF THE BRAVE, OLD SON. YOUR NECK OF THE WOODS...

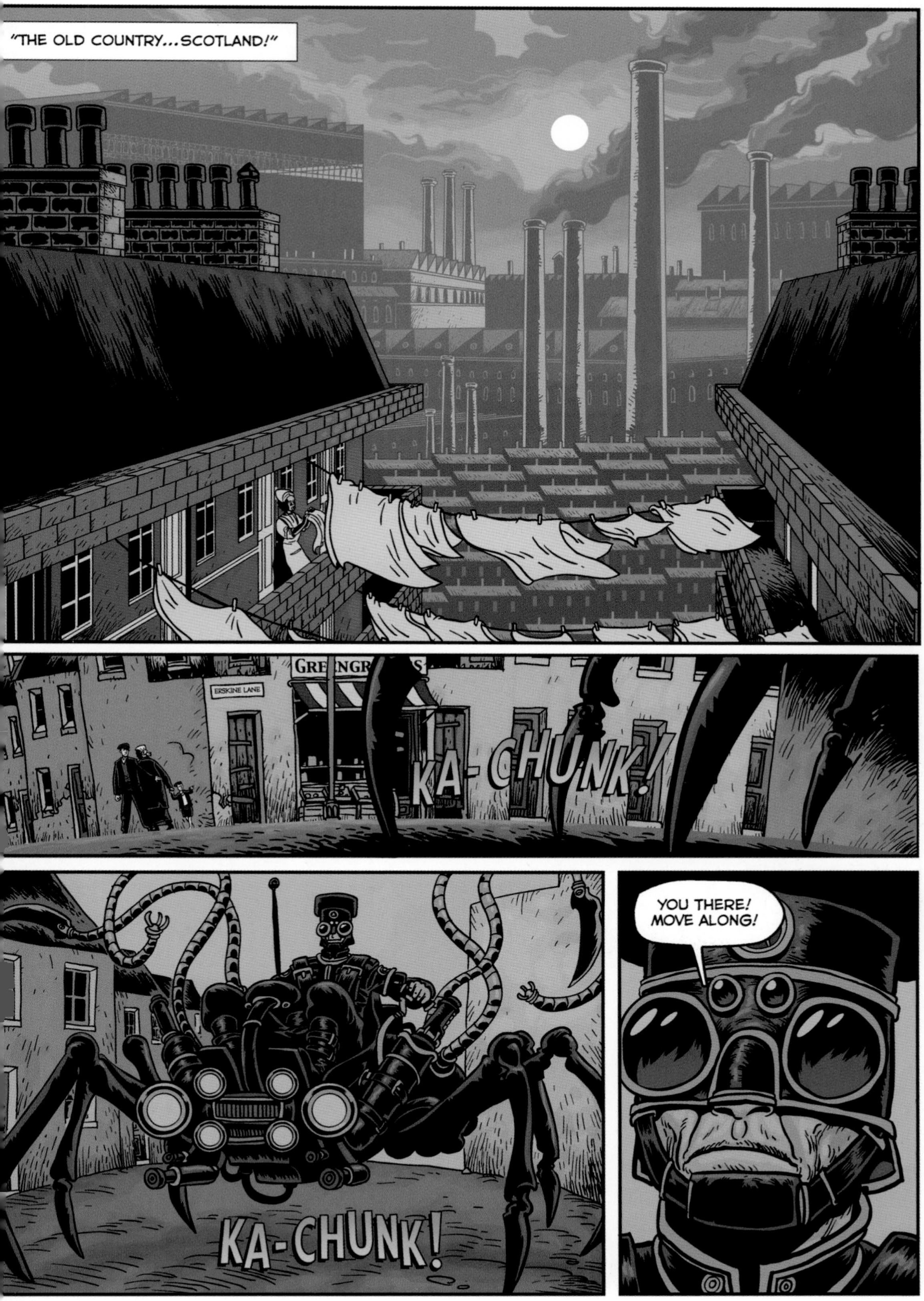
"THE OLD COUNTRY...SCOTLAND!"
ERSKINE LANE
KA-CHUNK!
KA-CHUNK!
YOU THERE! MOVE ALONG!

HE'S ROYAL ARTICULATED HUSSARS?

INDEED. THE GOVERNMENT ONLY DESPATCHES THEM TO EXTREME TROUBLE SPOTS IN THE EMPIRE. WHAT THE DEVIL ARE THEY DOING HERE?

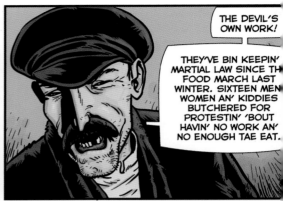

THE DEVIL'S OWN WORK!

THEY'VE BIN KEEPIN' MARTIAL LAW SINCE TH' FOOD MARCH LAST WINTER. SIXTEEN MEN WOMEN AN' KIDDIES BUTCHERED FOR PROTESTIN' 'BOUT HAVIN' NO WORK AN' NO ENOUGH TAE EAT.

AYE, THE PAPERS CALLED IT "BLOODY SUNDAY."

AN' THEY MADE US OUT TAE BE THE MONSTERS! SAID WE SMASHED UP FACTORIES, TORCHED TH'MILLS! ALL LIES!

Y'KNOW WE WORE OUR SUNDAY BEST TAE THE MARCH, TAE SHOW 'EM WE MEBBE POOR BUT WE'RE STILL PEOPLE, WI' PRIDE AN' SELF RESPEC

AN' THEY CUT 'EM TAE PIECES WI' HEAT RAYS AN' SABRES!

EASY, DAVY.

BUT... THAT'S OBSCENE! THIS IS GREAT BRITAIN, THE HEART OF EMPIRE!

AYE SUR, AN' IT'S A COLD HEART TAE BE SURE.

IF THERE'S A PRICE TAE PAY FOR Y'MACHINES AN' COMFY LIVIN', WE'RE PAYIN' IT IN FULL.

WE'RE HERE.

KLEY & Co. Ltd BER PRODUCTS

PRINTERS PR

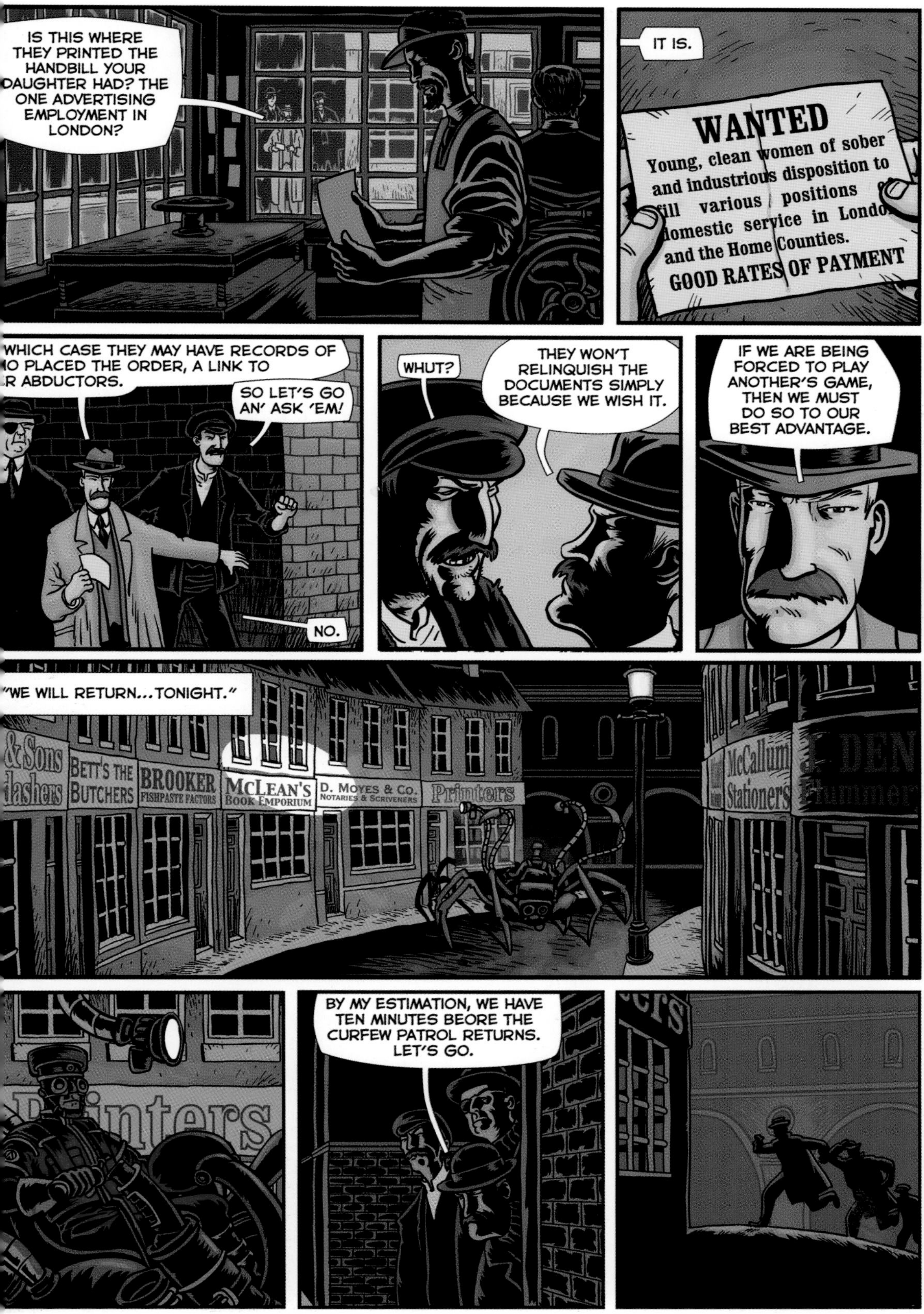
IS THIS WHERE THEY PRINTED THE HANDBILL YOUR DAUGHTER HAD? THE ONE ADVERTISING EMPLOYMENT IN LONDON?
IT IS.
WANTED
Young, clean women of sober and industrious disposition to fill various positions domestic service in London and the Home Counties.
GOOD RATES OF PAYMENT
WHICH CASE THEY MAY HAVE RECORDS OF O PLACED THE ORDER, A LINK TO R ABDUCTORS.
SO LET'S GO AN' ASK 'EM!
NO.
WHUT?
THEY WON'T RELINQUISH THE DOCUMENTS SIMPLY BECAUSE WE WISH IT.
IF WE ARE BEING FORCED TO PLAY ANOTHER'S GAME, THEN WE MUST DO SO TO OUR BEST ADVANTAGE.
"WE WILL RETURN...TONIGHT."
&Sons dashers
BETT'S THE BUTCHERS
BROOKER FISHPASTE FACTORS
McLEAN'S BOOK EMPORIUM
D. MOYES & CO. NOTARIES & SCRIVENERS
Printers
McCallum Stationers
Printers
BY MY ESTIMATION, WE HAVE TEN MINUTES BEORE THE CURFEW PATROL RETURNS. LET'S GO.

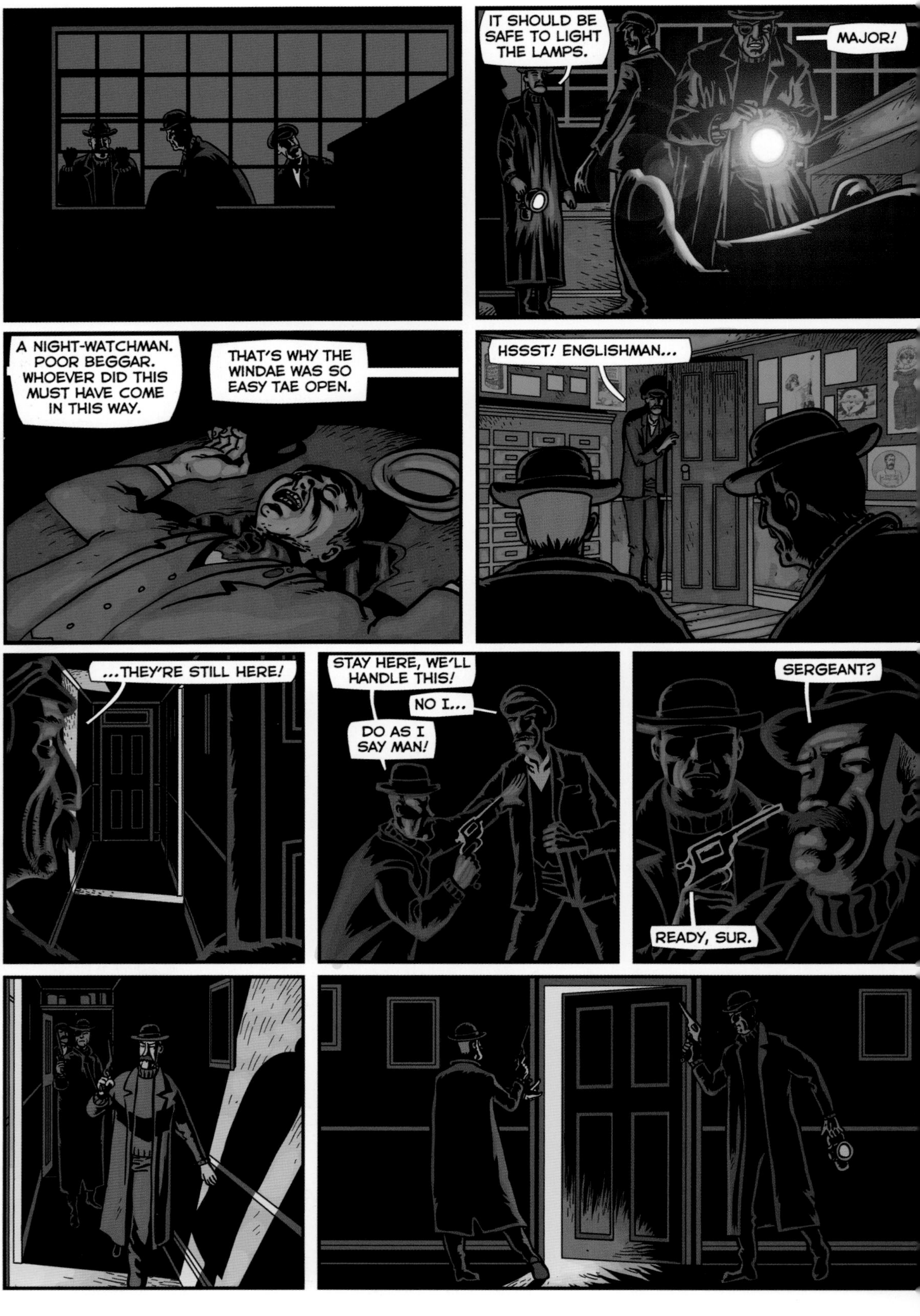
IT SHOULD BE SAFE TO LIGHT THE LAMPS.
MAJOR!
A NIGHT-WATCHMAN. POOR BEGGAR. WHOEVER DID THIS MUST HAVE COME IN THIS WAY.
THAT'S WHY THE WINDAE WAS SO EASY TAE OPEN.
HSSST! ENGLISHMAN...
...THEY'RE STILL HERE!
STAY HERE, WE'LL HANDLE THIS!
NO I...
DO AS I SAY MAN!
SERGEANT?
READY, SUR.

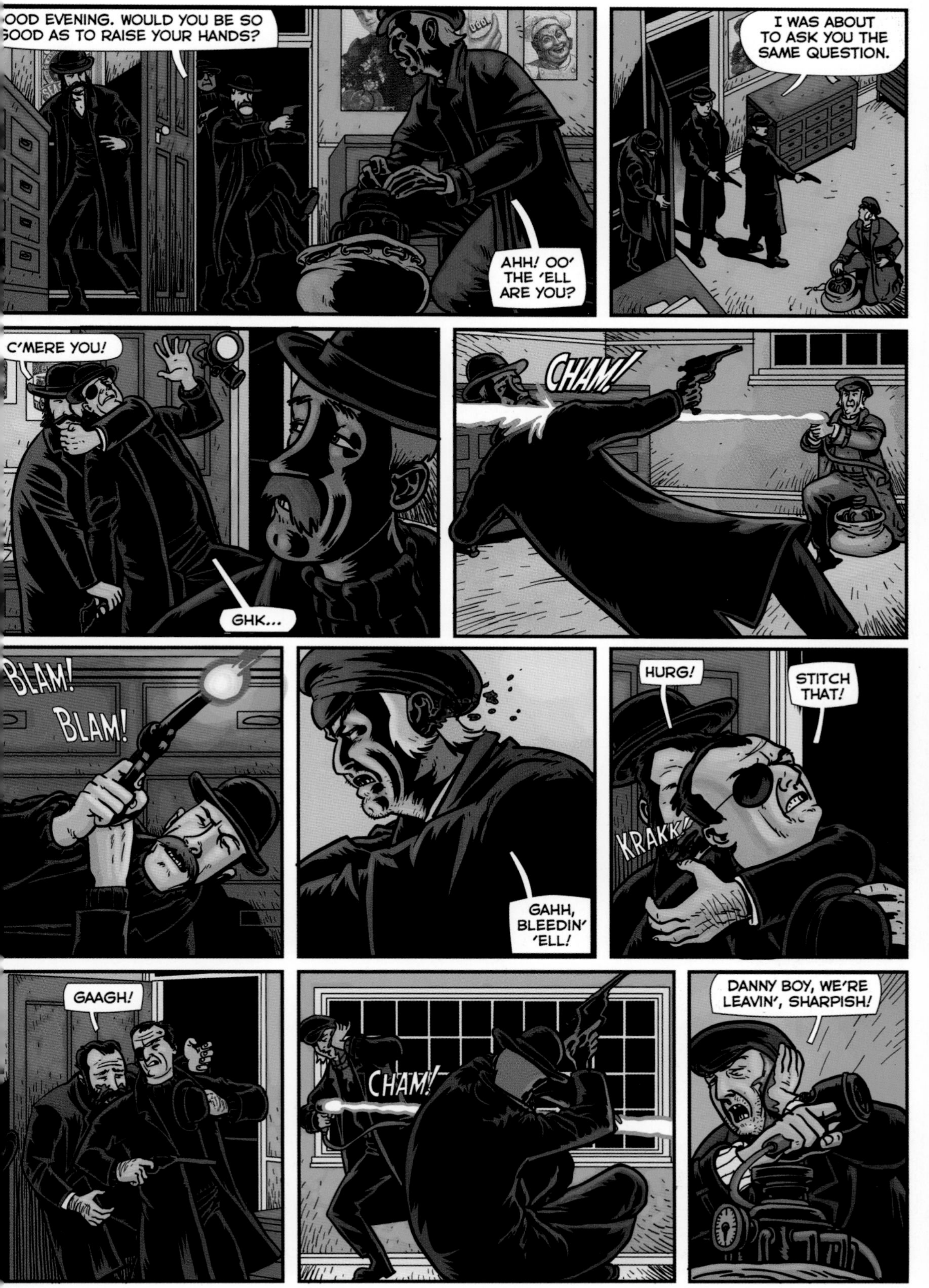
OOD EVENING. WOULD YOU BE SO GOOD AS TO RAISE YOUR HANDS?
AHH! OO' THE 'ELL ARE YOU?
I WAS ABOUT TO ASK YOU THE SAME QUESTION.
C'MERE YOU!
GHK...
CHAM!
BLAM!
BLAM!
GAHH, BLEEDIN' 'ELL!
HURG!
STITCH THAT!
KRAKK!
GAAGH!
CHAM!
DANNY BOY, WE'RE LEAVIN', SHARPISH!

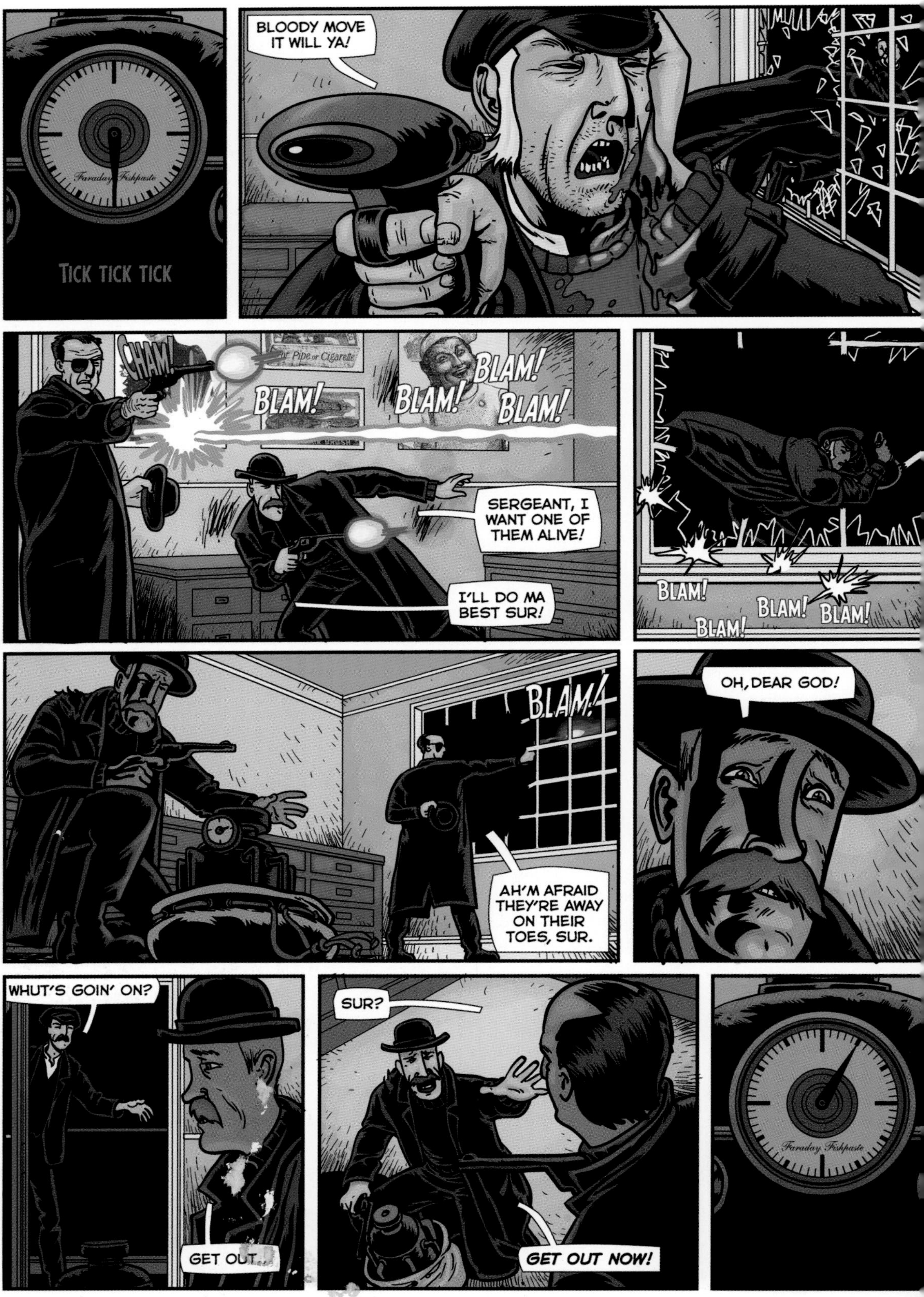
Faraday Fishpaste
TICK TICK TICK
BLOODY MOVE IT WILL YA!
CHAM!
BLAM!
BLAM!
BLAM!
BLAM!
SERGEANT, I WANT ONE OF THEM ALIVE!
I'LL DO MA BEST SUR!
BLAM!
BLAM!
BLAM!
BLAM!
BLAM!
AH'M AFRAID THEY'RE AWAY ON THEIR TOES, SUR.
OH, DEAR GOD!
WHUT'S GOIN' ON?
GET OUT...
SUR?
GET OUT NOW!
Faraday Fishpaste

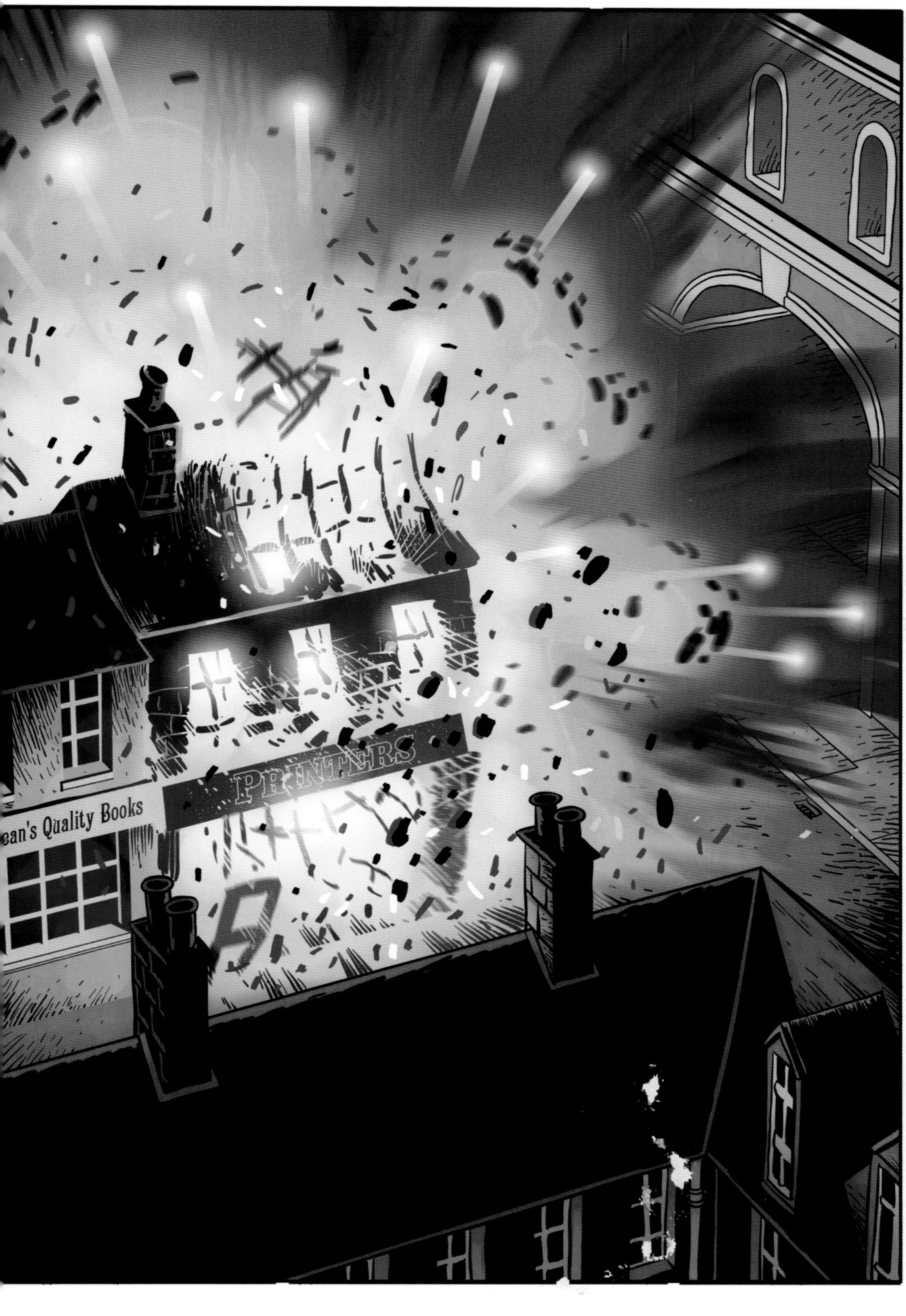
ean's Quality Books
PRINTERS

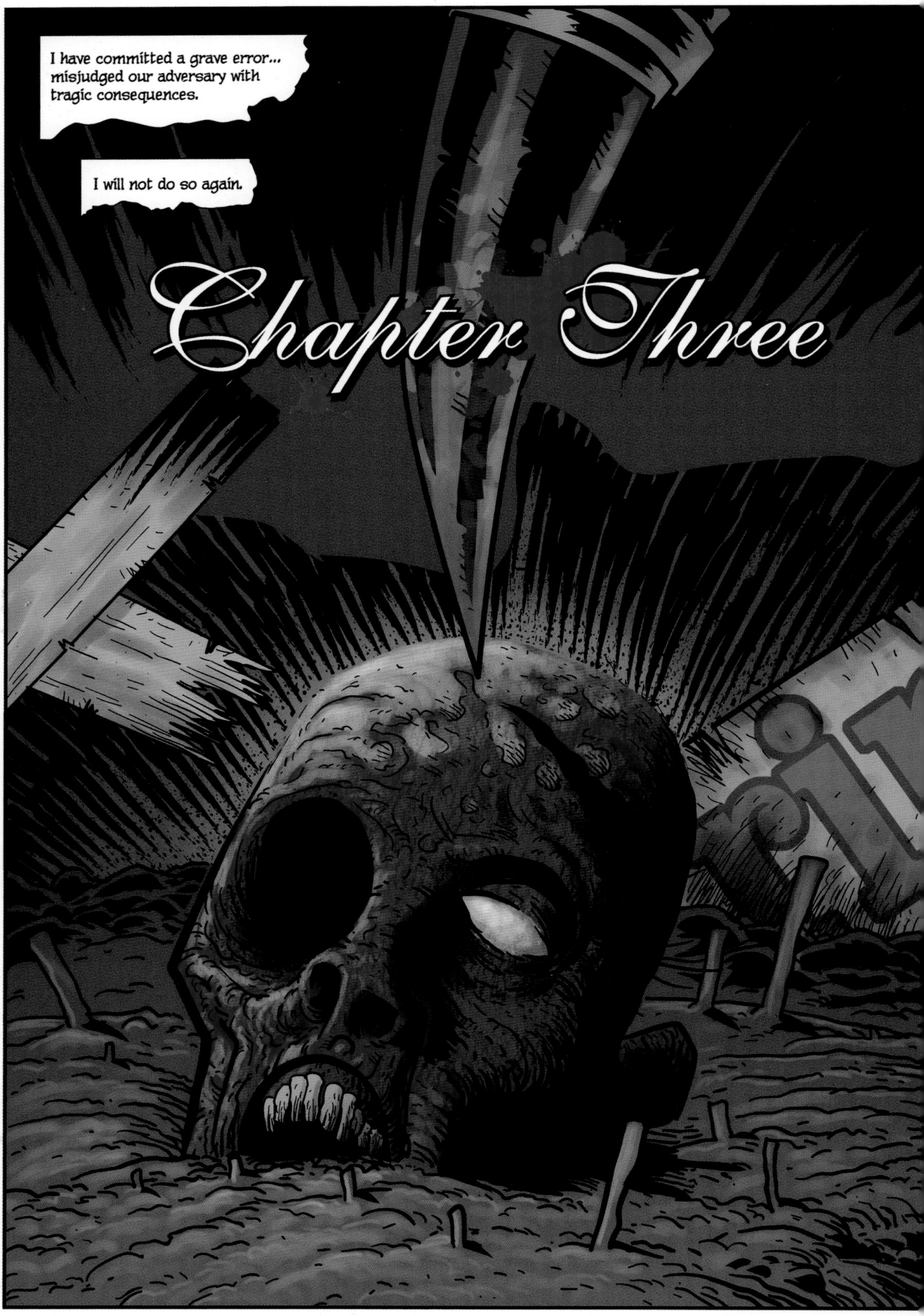
I have committed a grave error... misjudged our adversary with tragic consequences.
I will not do so again.
Chapter Three

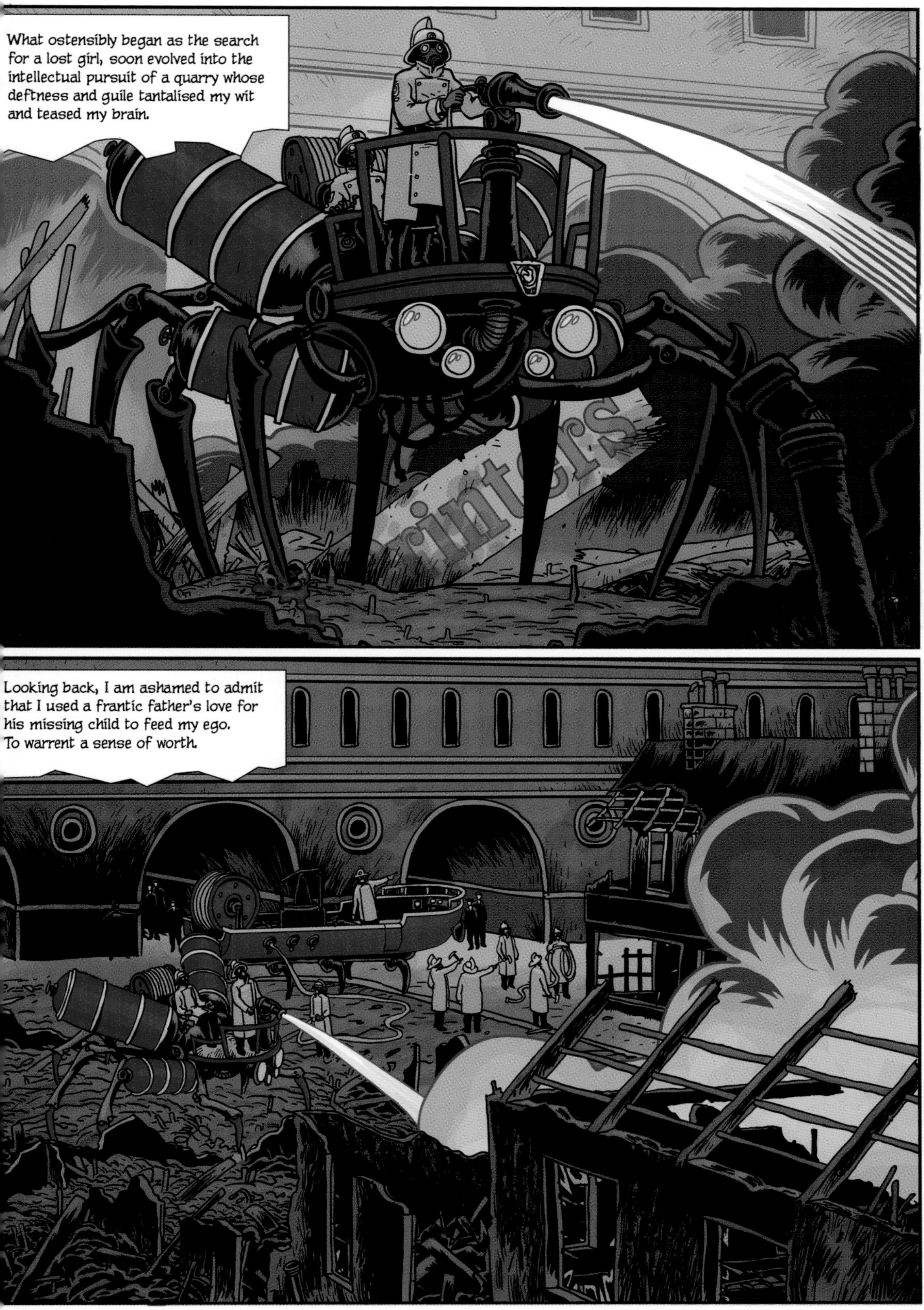
What ostensibly began as the search for a lost girl, soon evolved into the intellectual pursuit of a quarry whose deftness and guile tantalised my wit and teased my brain.
Looking back, I am ashamed to admit that I used a frantic father's love for his missing child to feed my ego. To warrent a sense of worth.

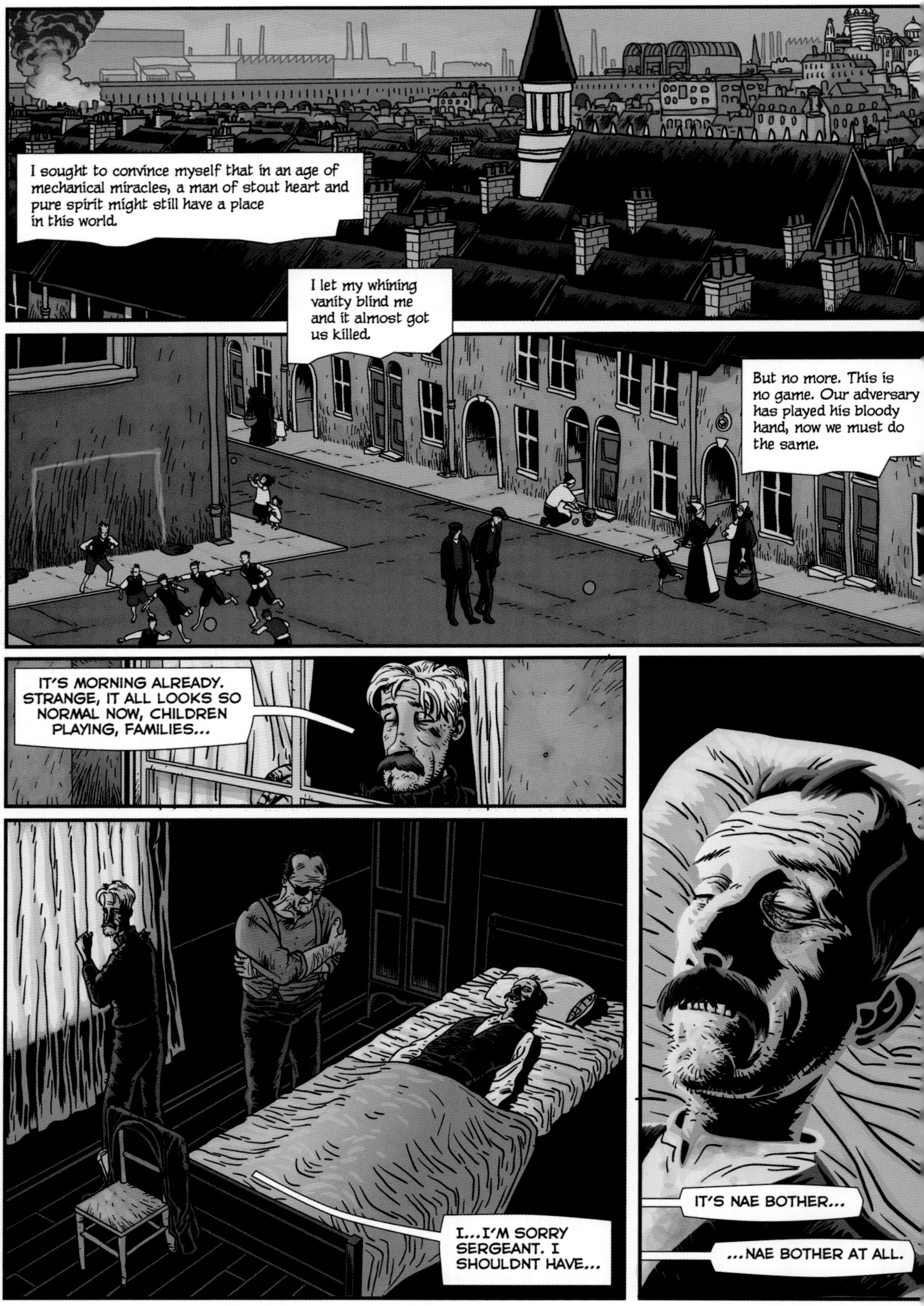
I sought to convince myself that in an age of mechanical miracles, a man of stout heart and pure spirit might still have a place in this world.
I let my whining vanity blind me and it almost got us killed.
But no more. This is no game. Our adversary has played his bloody hand, now we must do the same.
IT'S MORNING ALREADY. STRANGE, IT ALL LOOKS SO NORMAL NOW, CHILDREN PLAYING, FAMILIES...
I...I'M SORRY SERGEANT. I SHOULDNT HAVE...
IT'S NAE BOTHER...
...NAE BOTHER AT ALL.

I'M SORRY FOR YOUR LOSS, SERGEANT, HE WAS A FINE MAN.

AYE, HE WAS ALSO A CONTRARY BUGGER. TOO FOND O'THE BOTTLE AN TOO QUICK WI' HIS FISTS, BUT HE HAD A GOOD HEART.

WHAT WILL HAPPEN NOW?

ME AN MARIE... HIS MISSUS, WE'LL WASH AN' DRESS 'IM FER THE FUNERAL. PUT 'IM IN HIS SUNDAY BEST.

WON'T YOU REQUIRE A DEATH CERTIFICATE FIRST?

NAW. THE AMOUNT OF FOLKS DYIN' UP HERE, YON DOCTOR'LL GI' US A SCRIP JUST ON OUR SAY SO.

HE'LL NO BE FUSSED ABOUT SEEIN' ANOTHER CORPSE.

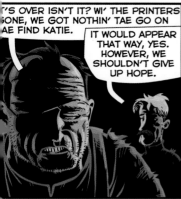

IT'S OVER ISN'T IT? WI' THE PRINTERS GONE, WE GOT NOTHIN' TAE GO ON TAE FIND KATIE.

IT WOULD APPEAR THAT WAY, YES. HOWEVER, WE SHOULDN'T GIVE UP HOPE.

HOPE...AYE.

WELL, I'D BEST SEE TAE ME AN MINE.

CAN I HELP IN ANY WAY?

AYE, THANK YOU SIR. COULD Y'GO LIGHT A FIRE IN THE GRATE DOWN-STAIRS, BOIL SOME WATER FER DAVY'S WASH?

CERTAINLY.

THERE'S A PAPER IN MA POCKET, TAKE IT. IT'LL DO F'KINDLIN.

GOOD GOD ALMIGHTY!!

June 20th, 1900 Price 3d

DOG-EA

SERGEANT, WHEN DID YOU BUY THIS?

A FEW DAYS AGO, JUST BEFORE WE BOARDED THE AIRSHIP BACK IN LONDON. WHY?

TAKE A LOOK AT THE PICTURE, MAN!

GOD SAVE THE QUEEN! On Sale Every Wed

TIT-BITS

All the News of the Day, Told in Short Words for the Lower

DULWICH RED RETUR

YOUNG W
BODIES
THE T

TERROR swep
Thames last nigh
numerous young
washed up on th

BLOOD SU
BACK SA
WAR

MARTIAN V
(pictured le
salvage reclar
End, was the
He is convin
terrifying p
return of D
"Vampyre"
lives of s
dubious m

 rian War Veteran Ned stands at the spot where he discovered the remains of the young women.

IN THE BACKGROUND.

RECOGNISE ANY FAMILIAR FACES?

MISTER COUGHLY AND MISTER DRAVOTT ARE HERE TO SEE YOU, SIR DAVENPORT.

THANK YOU HERBERT. YOU'VE MADE GOOD TIME GENTLEMEN. YOU HAD A COMFORTABLE FLIGHT?

ALL THE BETTER F'BEIN' IN FIRST CLASS SIR, YES. THEM TICKETS WAS MUCH APPRECIATED.

THE LEAST I COULD DO TO REWARD YOUR GOOD WORK.

SPEAKING OF WHICH, ALL WENT WELL I TRUST? NOTHING UNTOWARD OCCURRED?

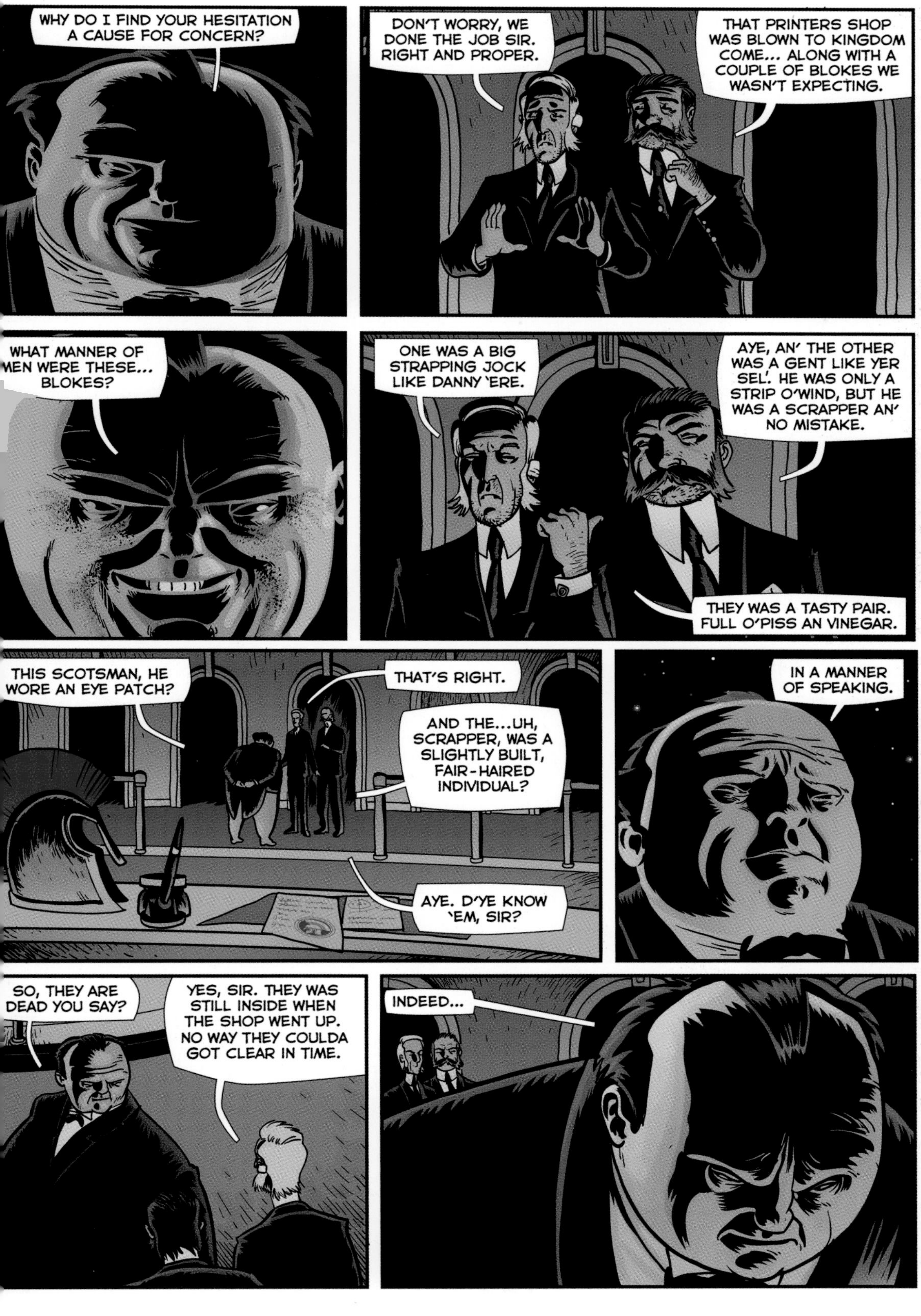
WHY DO I FIND YOUR HESITATION A CAUSE FOR CONCERN?
DON'T WORRY, WE DONE THE JOB SIR. RIGHT AND PROPER.
THAT PRINTERS SHOP WAS BLOWN TO KINGDOM COME... ALONG WITH A COUPLE OF BLOKES WE WASN'T EXPECTING.
WHAT MANNER OF MEN WERE THESE... BLOKES?
ONE WAS A BIG STRAPPING JOCK LIKE DANNY 'ERE.
AYE, AN' THE OTHER WAS A GENT LIKE YER SEL'. HE WAS ONLY A STRIP O'WIND, BUT HE WAS A SCRAPPER AN' NO MISTAKE.
THEY WAS A TASTY PAIR. FULL O'PISS AN VINEGAR.
THIS SCOTSMAN, HE WORE AN EYE PATCH?
THAT'S RIGHT.
AND THE...UH, SCRAPPER, WAS A SLIGHTLY BUILT, FAIR-HAIRED INDIVIDUAL?
AYE. D'YE KNOW 'EM, SIR?
IN A MANNER OF SPEAKING.
SO, THEY ARE DEAD YOU SAY?
YES, SIR. THEY WAS STILL INSIDE WHEN THE SHOP WENT UP. NO WAY THEY COULDA GOT CLEAR IN TIME.
INDEED...

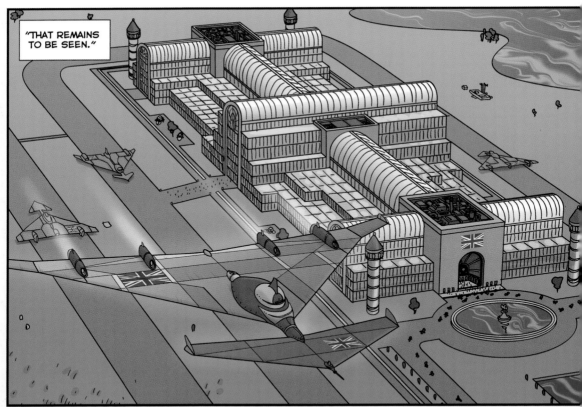

"THAT REMAINS TO BE SEEN."

CABBIE!

THE EAST END, MY GOOD MAN. WALFORD VIADUCT AND DON'T SPARE THE HORSEPOWER!

RIGHTCHOO ARE GUV'NOR.

IF THIS ITEM IS CORRECT, THIS OLD NED CHARACTER IS A REGULAR PATRON AT THE QUEEN BESS PUBLIC HOUSE.

EVEN IF HE ISN'T THERE PRESENTLY, I DARE SAY THE LOCALS MAY KNOW HIS WHEREABOUTS?

AYE...

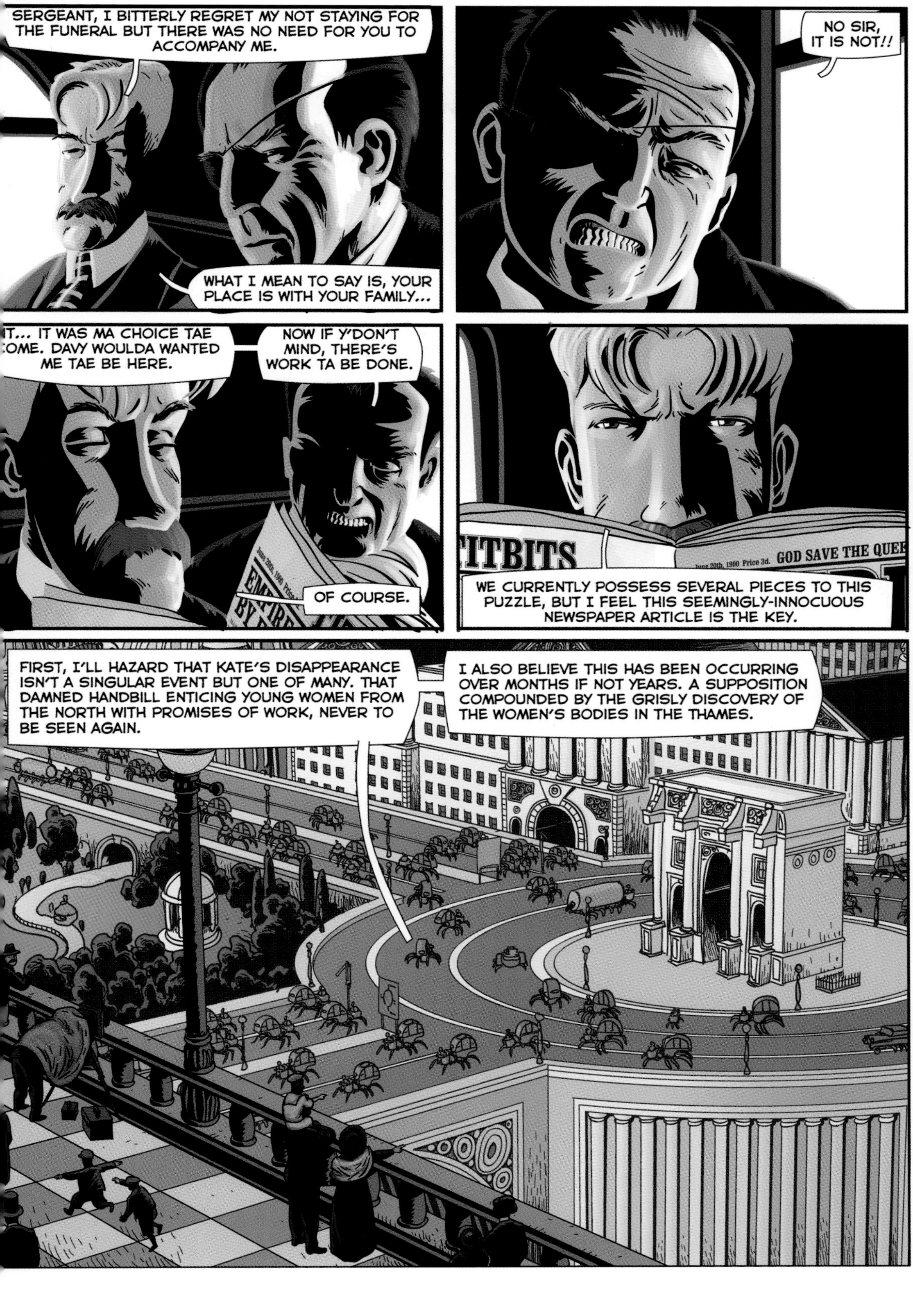
SERGEANT, I BITTERLY REGRET MY NOT STAYING FOR THE FUNERAL BUT THERE WAS NO NEED FOR YOU TO ACCOMPANY ME.
WHAT I MEAN TO SAY IS, YOUR PLACE IS WITH YOUR FAMILY...
NO SIR, IT IS NOT!!
IT... IT WAS MA CHOICE TAE COME. DAVY WOULDA WANTED ME TAE BE HERE.
NOW IF Y'DON'T MIND, THERE'S WORK TA BE DONE.
OF COURSE.
ITBITS
June 20th, 1900 Price 3d. GOD SAVE THE QUE
WE CURRENTLY POSSESS SEVERAL PIECES TO THIS PUZZLE, BUT I FEEL THIS SEEMINGLY-INNOCUOUS NEWSPAPER ARTICLE IS THE KEY.
FIRST, I'LL HAZARD THAT KATE'S DISAPPEARANCE ISN'T A SINGULAR EVENT BUT ONE OF MANY. THAT DAMNED HANDBILL ENTICING YOUNG WOMEN FROM THE NORTH WITH PROMISES OF WORK, NEVER TO BE SEEN AGAIN.
I ALSO BELIEVE THIS HAS BEEN OCCURRING OVER MONTHS IF NOT YEARS. A SUPPOSITION COMPOUNDED BY THE GRISLY DISCOVERY OF THE WOMEN'S BODIES IN THE THAMES.

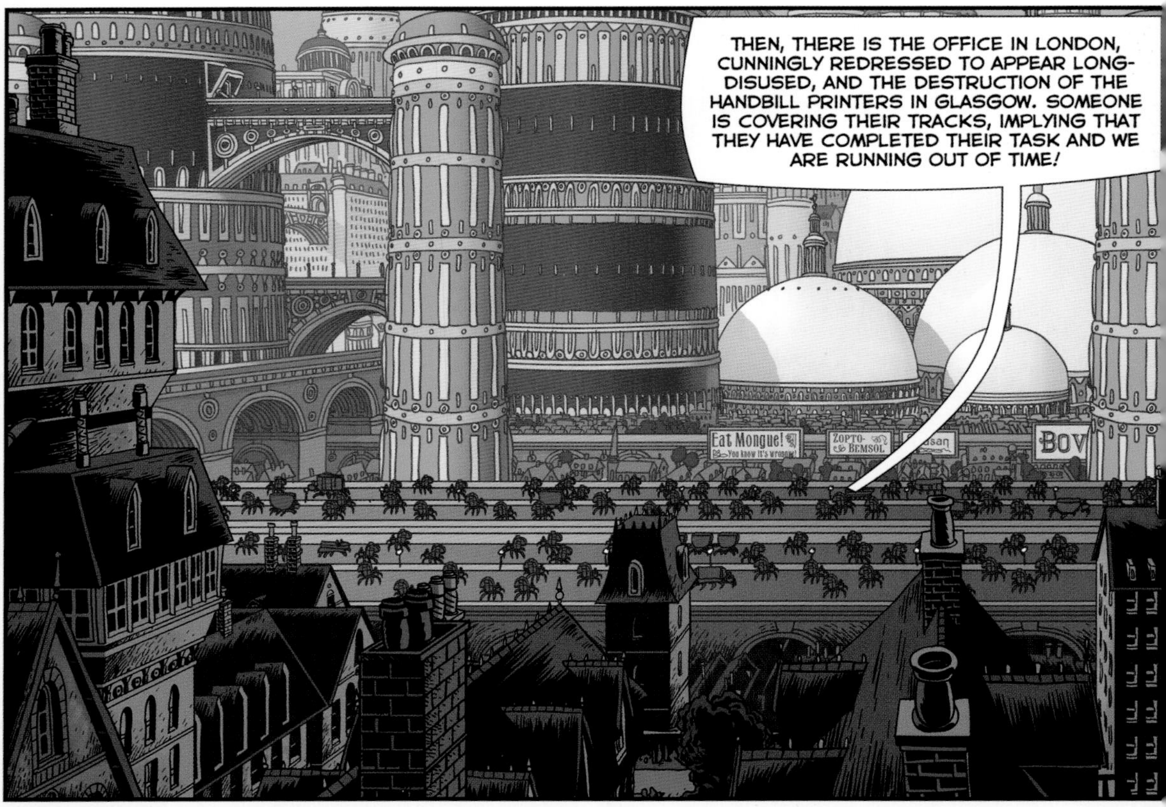
THEN, THERE IS THE OFFICE IN LONDON, CUNNINGLY REDRESSED TO APPEAR LONG-DISUSED, AND THE DESTRUCTION OF THE HANDBILL PRINTERS IN GLASGOW. SOMEONE IS COVERING THEIR TRACKS, IMPLYING THAT THEY HAVE COMPLETED THEIR TASK AND WE ARE RUNNING OUT OF TIME!
Eat Mongue!
ZOPTO-BEMSOL
BOV

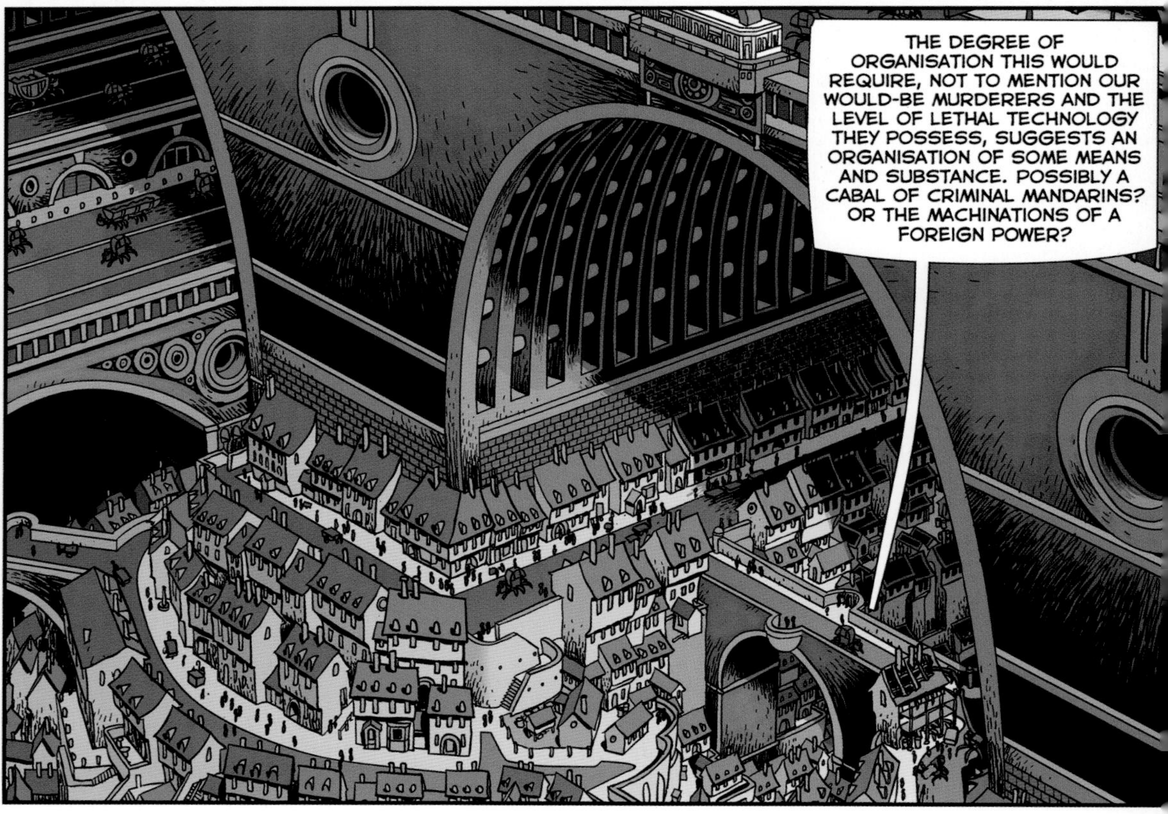
THE DEGREE OF ORGANISATION THIS WOULD REQUIRE, NOT TO MENTION OUR WOULD-BE MURDERERS AND THE LEVEL OF LETHAL TECHNOLOGY THEY POSSESS, SUGGESTS AN ORGANISATION OF SOME MEANS AND SUBSTANCE. POSSIBLY A CABAL OF CRIMINAL MANDARINS? OR THE MACHINATIONS OF A FOREIGN POWER?

WHICH MAKES IT ALL THE MORE IMPERATIVE THAT WE UNCOVER THE TRUTH... EXPOSE THIS NEFARIOUS AFFAIR TO THE LIGHT OF THE LAW.

WALFORD VIADUCT, GUV.

THANK YOU.

GREAT GOD ALMIGHTY!

WHAT ON EARTH HAPPENED HERE?

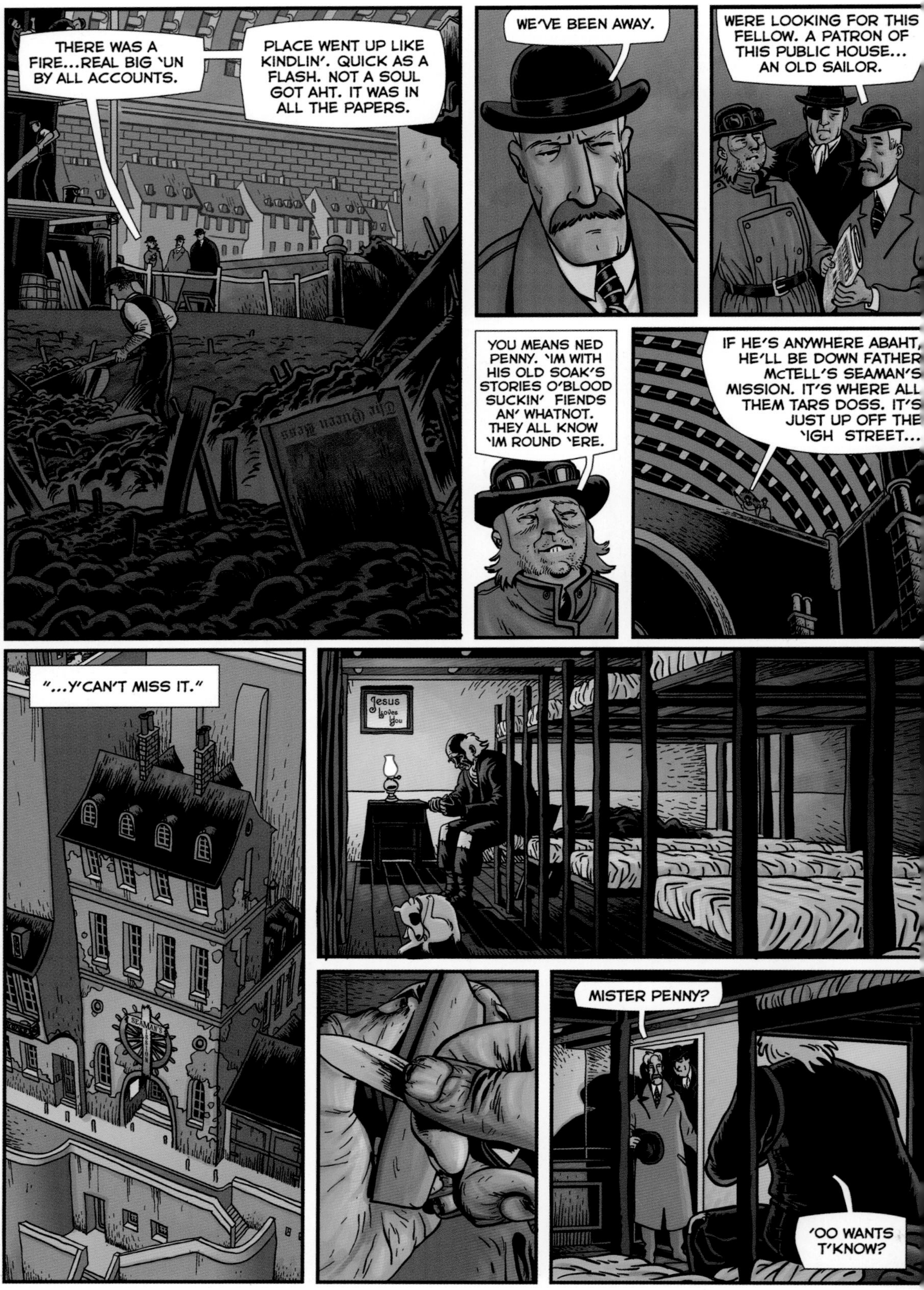
THERE WAS A FIRE...REAL BIG 'UN BY ALL ACCOUNTS.
PLACE WENT UP LIKE KINDLIN'. QUICK AS A FLASH. NOT A SOUL GOT AHT. IT WAS IN ALL THE PAPERS.
WE'VE BEEN AWAY.
WERE LOOKING FOR THIS FELLOW. A PATRON OF THIS PUBLIC HOUSE... AN OLD SAILOR.
YOU MEANS NED PENNY. 'IM WITH HIS OLD SOAK'S STORIES O'BLOOD SUCKIN' FIENDS AN' WHATNOT. THEY ALL KNOW 'IM ROUND 'ERE.
IF HE'S ANYWHERE ABAHT, HE'LL BE DOWN FATHER McTELL'S SEAMAN'S MISSION. IT'S WHERE ALL THEM TARS DOSS. IT'S JUST UP OFF THE 'IGH STREET...
"...Y'CAN'T MISS IT."
SEAMAN'S
Jesus Loves You
MISTER PENNY?
'OO WANTS T'KNOW?

MY NAME IS ROBERT AUTUMN, THIS IS MY MAN, MISTER CURRIE, WE'RE HERE TO --

Y'ERE ABOUT THE WOMEN, AINTCHA? WELL Y'CAN SOD OFF! I'M SICK O' YOU LOT TAKIN' THE MICKEY!

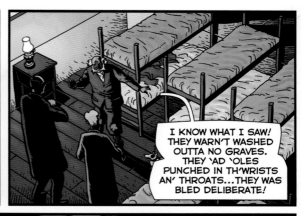

I KNOW WHAT I SAW! THEY WARN'T WASHED OUTTA NO GRAVES. THEY 'AD 'OLES PUNCHED IN TH'WRISTS AN' THROATS...THEY WAS BLED DELIBERATE!

I MAY BE OLD BUT I AIN'T ADDLED. THERE'S SUMMAT DARK AN' HEINOUS GOIN' ON BUT NO ONE BELIEVES ME...

WE BELIEVE YOU. IN FACT, WE BELIEVE THE BODIES YOU FOUND ARE BUT THE TIP OF A GRISLY ICEBERG.

Jesus Loves You

WE ARE INTENT ON EXPOSING THE TRUTH AND WE NEED YOUR HELP.

YOU TALKS LIKE AN OFFICER. WHAT WAS YOU? ARMY?

THE COLDSTREAM GUARDS. BOTH OF US.

SERGEANT, RIGHT? YOU GOT THE LOOK.

COLOUR SERGEANT, AYE. YOU TOO?

THA'S RIGHT. I WAS GUNNERY SERGEANT... ON THE THUNDERCHILD.

THE IRONCLAD? I THOUGHT SHE WAS LOST WITH ALL HANDS DURING THE WAR?

NO...NOT ALL.

YOU SHOULDA SEEN 'ER THAT DAY BY GOD...

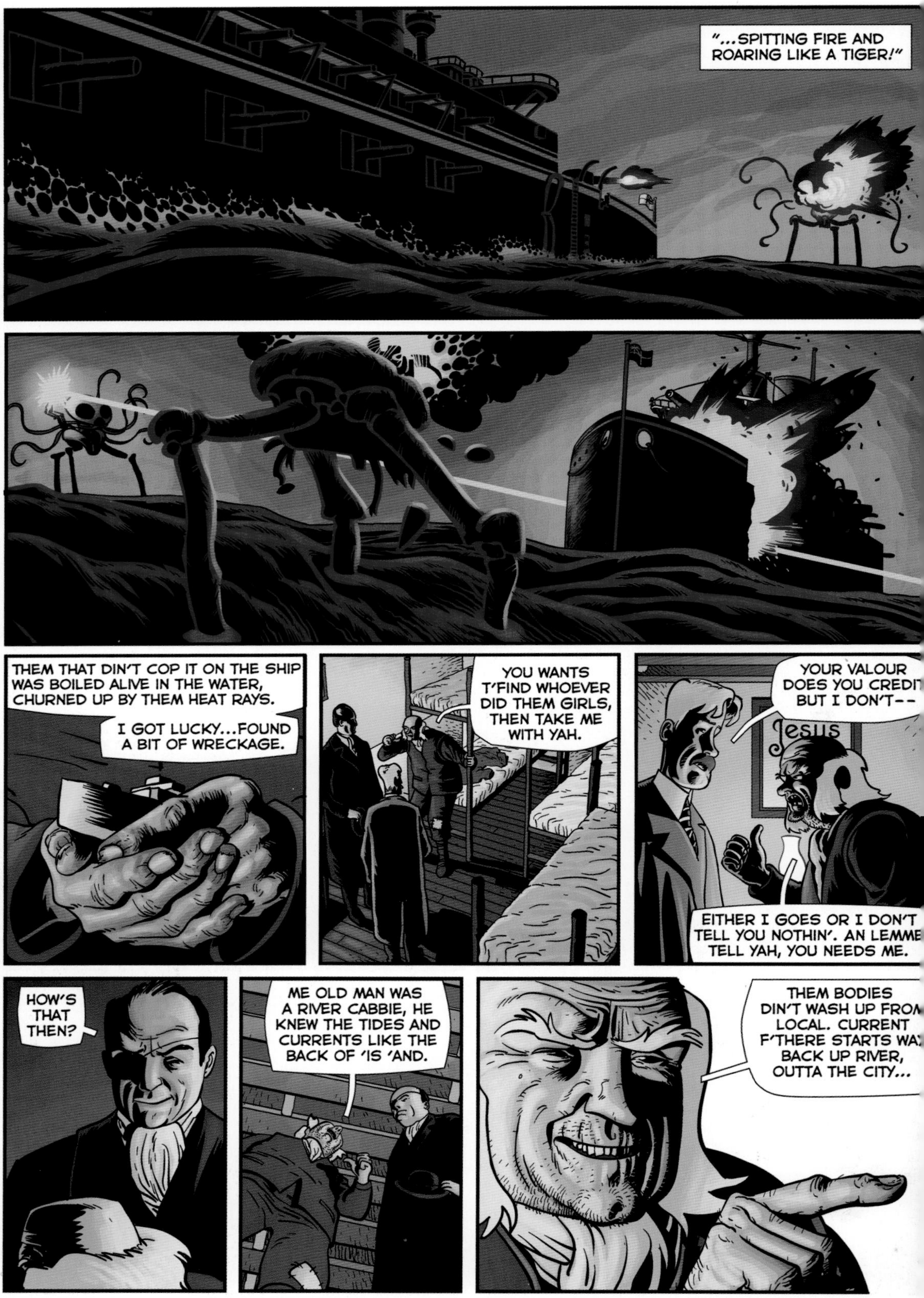
"...SPITTING FIRE AND ROARING LIKE A TIGER!"
THEM THAT DIN'T COP IT ON THE SHIP WAS BOILED ALIVE IN THE WATER, CHURNED UP BY THEM HEAT RAYS.
I GOT LUCKY...FOUND A BIT OF WRECKAGE.
YOU WANTS T'FIND WHOEVER DID THEM GIRLS, THEN TAKE ME WITH YAH.
YOUR VALOUR DOES YOU CREDIT BUT I DON'T--
JESUS
EITHER I GOES OR I DON'T TELL YOU NOTHIN'. AN LEMME TELL YAH, YOU NEEDS ME.
HOW'S THAT THEN?
ME OLD MAN WAS A RIVER CABBIE, HE KNEW THE TIDES AND CURRENTS LIKE THE BACK OF 'IS 'AND.
THEM BODIES DIN'T WASH UP FROM LOCAL. CURRENT F'THERE STARTS WAY BACK UP RIVER, OUTTA THE CITY...

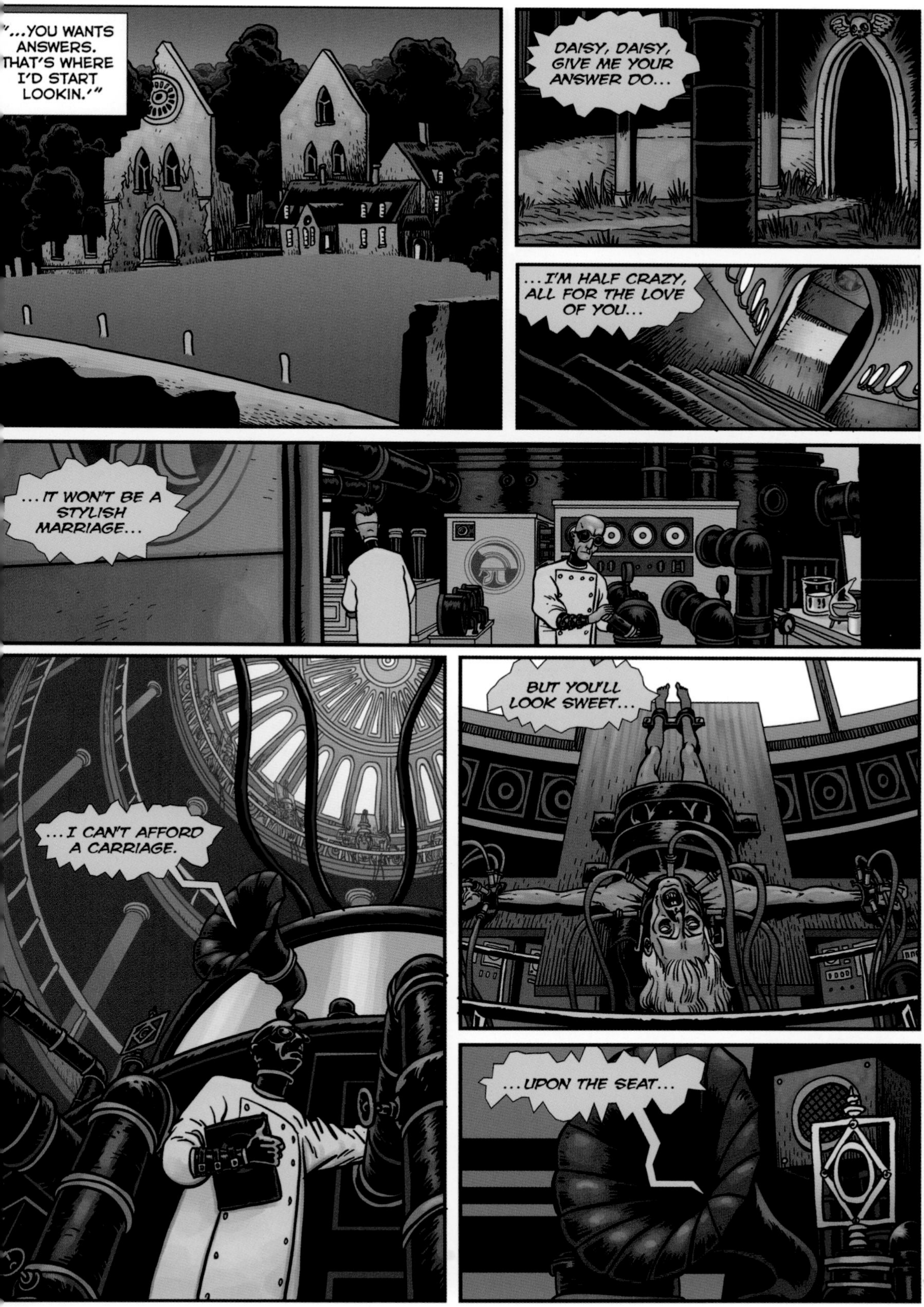
"...YOU WANTS ANSWERS. THAT'S WHERE I'D START LOOKIN.'"
DAISY, DAISY, GIVE ME YOUR ANSWER DO...
...I'M HALF CRAZY, ALL FOR THE LOVE OF YOU...
...IT WON'T BE A STYLISH MARRIAGE...
...I CAN'T AFFORD A CARRIAGE.
BUT YOU'LL LOOK SWEET...
...UPON THE SEAT...

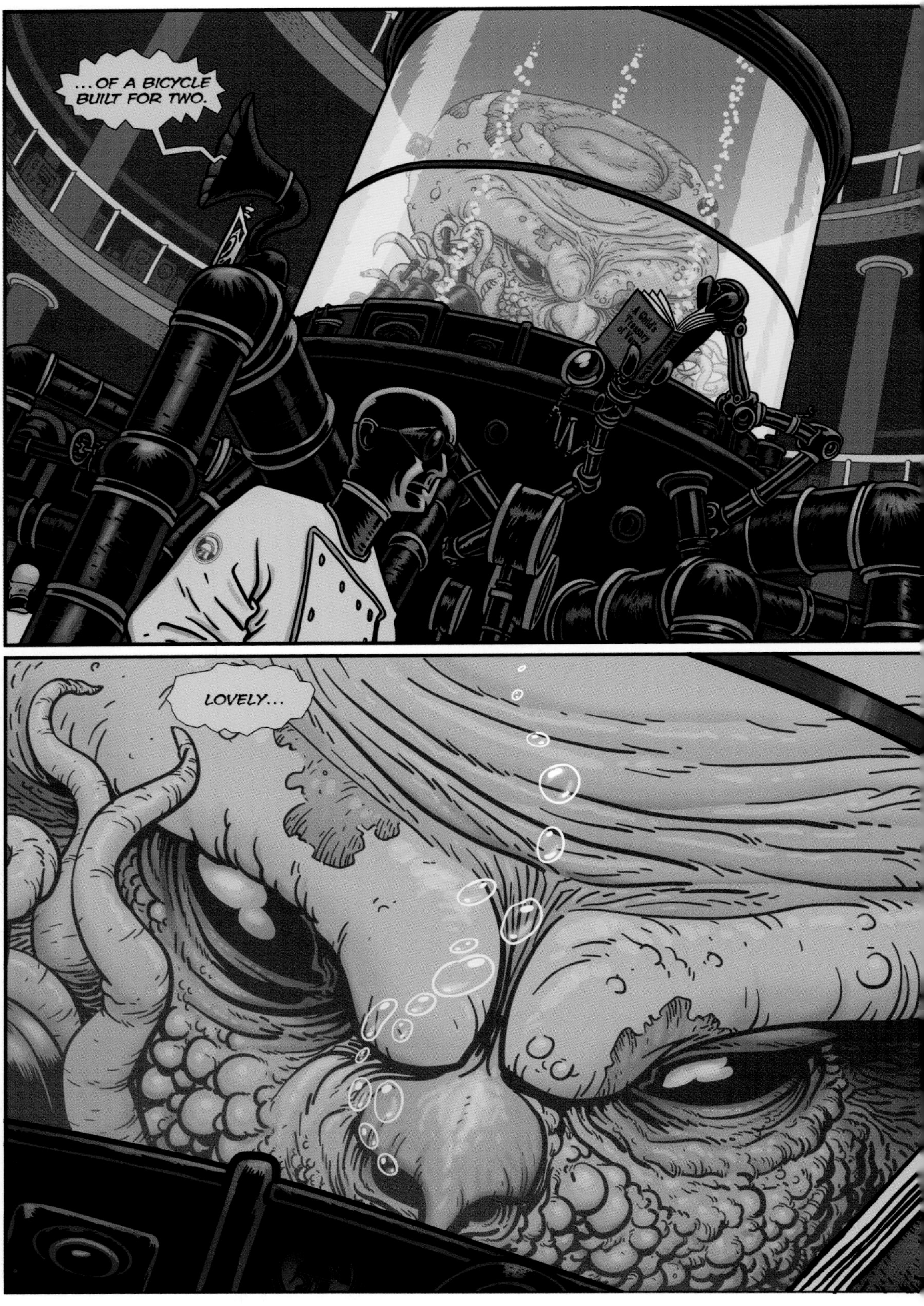
...OF A BICYCLE BUILT FOR TWO.
A Child's Treasury of Verse
LOVELY...

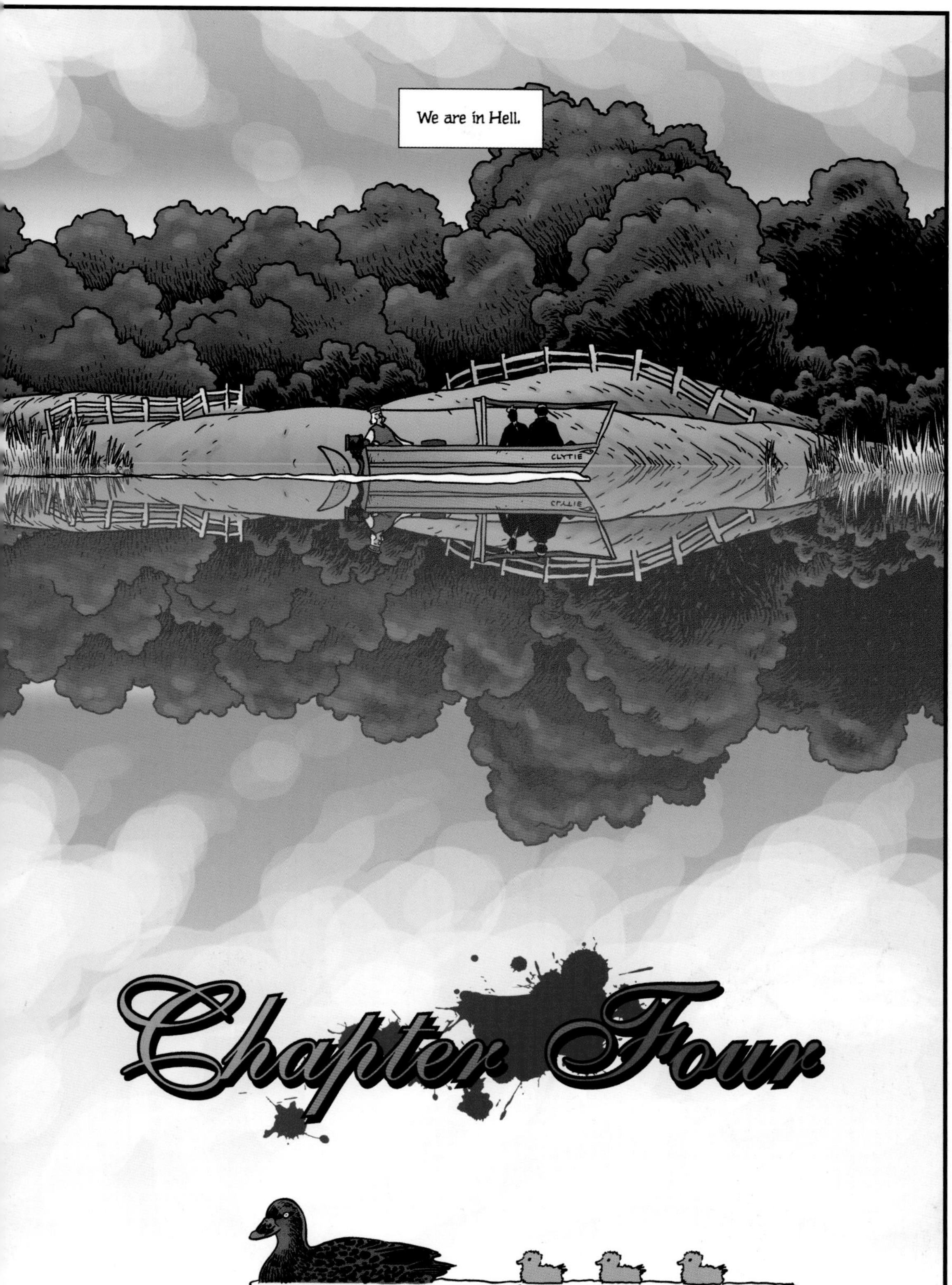
We are in Hell.
CLYTIE
Chapter Four

There is a heart of darkness in this green and pleasant land. A wretched purgatory where the weak, poor and dispossessed are a commodity, abused and exploited for the luxury and providence of others.

We have become as indifferent to their plight as the remorseless Martian technology upon which we are so dependent.

Alien machineries oiled with human blood and bitter tears.

I consider myself a simple man, a good soldier with few aspirations beyond defending my country and its virtues...dignity, truth, honour.

How hollow they sound now.

All that matters presently is the search for a lost soul. To discover the fate of Sergeant Currie's missing niece Katherine.

However, Mister Penny's chilling discovery of the exsanguinated bodies of several young women washed up on the Thames mud flats does not bode well.

He insists it is the work of Old Varney, a Penny Dreadful nosferatu of London folklore.

These days though, I find the monsters of this world are all too human.

GOOD LORD! LOOK THERE...

RED WEED.

I KNEW THEY CULTIVATED IT BUT NOT ON SUCH A SCALE!

LOOKS LIKE A FIELD O'BLOOD.

THEY SAY IT ACCIDENTALLY CAME OVER WITH THE MARTIANS...IN THEIR CYLINDERS. JUST A FEW STRAY SEEDS.

NOW THEY FARM IT BECAUSE ITS OIL IS THE ONLY LUBRICANT THE MARTIAN-DERIVED TECHNOLOGY WILL TOLERATE.

SOUNDS LIKE NO ACCIDENT TAE ME!

WE'S GOTTA CHANGE COURSE, GO UP THATAWAY.

ARE YOU CERTAIN? HOW CAN YOU TELL?

LOOK AT TH'BANK. S'WORN DARN BY THE CURRENT MORE'N T'OTHER 'CAUSE IT'S STRONGER, SEE.

I RECKON THEM BODIES WAS CARRIED DARN RIVER BY TH'CURRENT WOT STARTED 'ERE ROUNDABOUTS.

HE'S RIGHT, SUR...

WE'RE GETTIN' CLOSE.

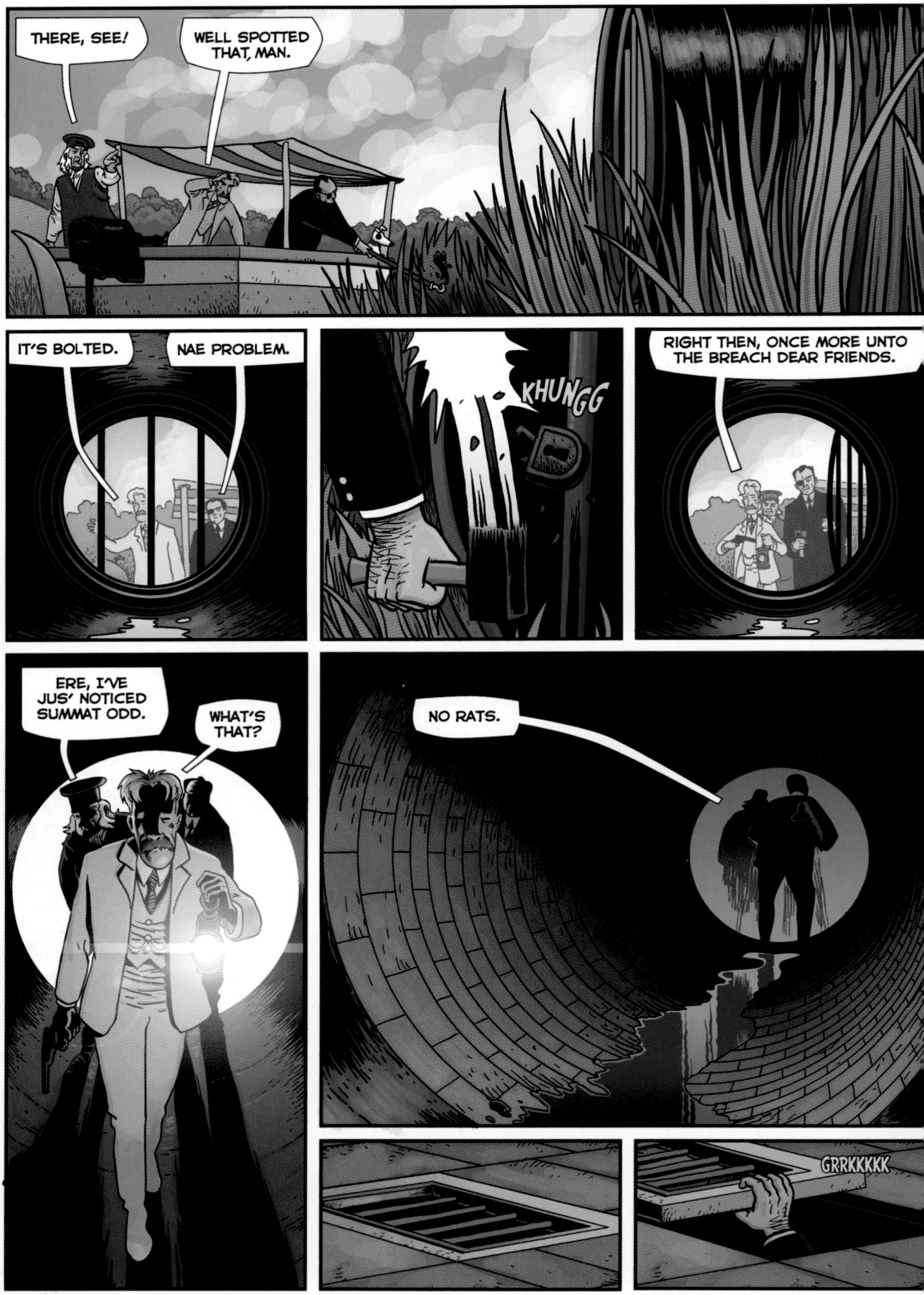
THERE, SEE!
WELL SPOTTED THAT, MAN.
IT'S BOLTED.
NAE PROBLEM.
KHUNGG
RIGHT THEN, ONCE MORE UNTO THE BREACH DEAR FRIENDS.
ERE, I'VE JUS' NOTICED SUMMAT ODD.
WHAT'S THAT?
NO RATS.
GRRKKKKK

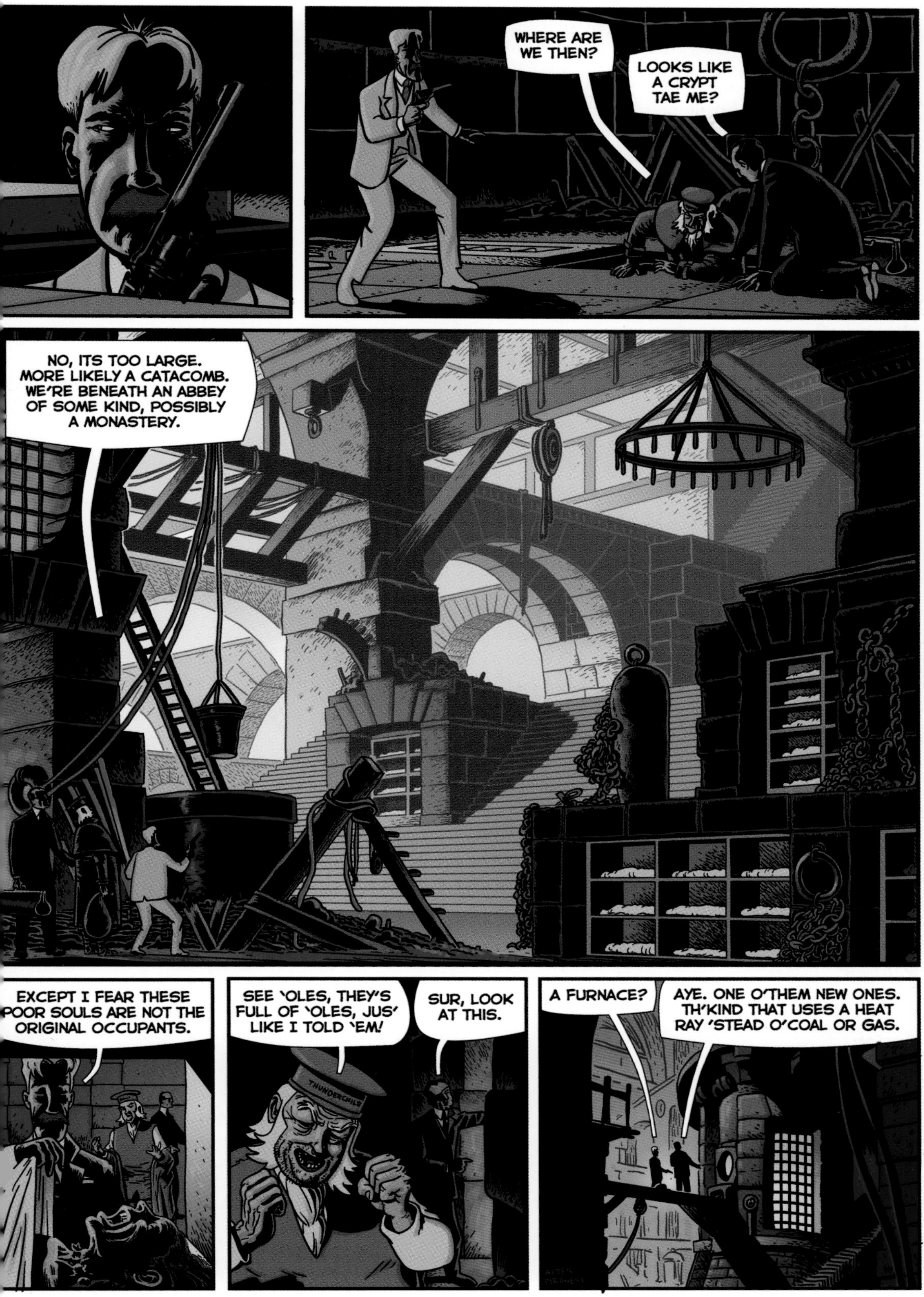
WHERE ARE WE THEN?
LOOKS LIKE A CRYPT TAE ME?
NO, ITS TOO LARGE. MORE LIKELY A CATACOMB. WE'RE BENEATH AN ABBEY OF SOME KIND, POSSIBLY A MONASTERY.
EXCEPT I FEAR THESE POOR SOULS ARE NOT THE ORIGINAL OCCUPANTS.
SEE 'OLES, THEY'S FULL OF 'OLES, JUS' LIKE I TOLD 'EM!
SUR, LOOK AT THIS.
A FURNACE?
AYE. ONE O'THEM NEW ONES. TH'KIND THAT USES A HEAT RAY 'STEAD O'COAL OR GAS.

SEE HERE. THESE GOUGES ARE FRESH. THIS DEVICE HAS ONLY RECENTLY BEEN INSTALLED.

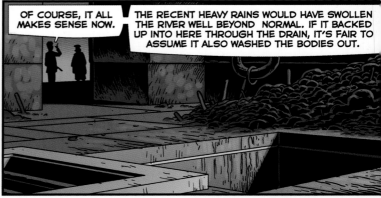

OF COURSE, IT ALL MAKES SENSE NOW.

THE RECENT HEAVY RAINS WOULD HAVE SWOLLEN THE RIVER WELL BEYOND NORMAL. IF IT BACKED UP INTO HERE THROUGH THE DRAIN, IT'S FAIR TO ASSUME IT ALSO WASHED THE BODIES OUT.

THEY WERE THEN CARRIED DOWN STREAM AND BEACHED ON THE MUD BANK WHEN THE TIDE RECEDED.

SO NOW THEY BURNS 'EM INSTEAD?

EXACTLY. SERGEANT, WE SHOULD-- SERGEANT?

OH, DEAR LORD.

THIS WHERE THEY KEPT 'EM. LIKE ANIMALS.

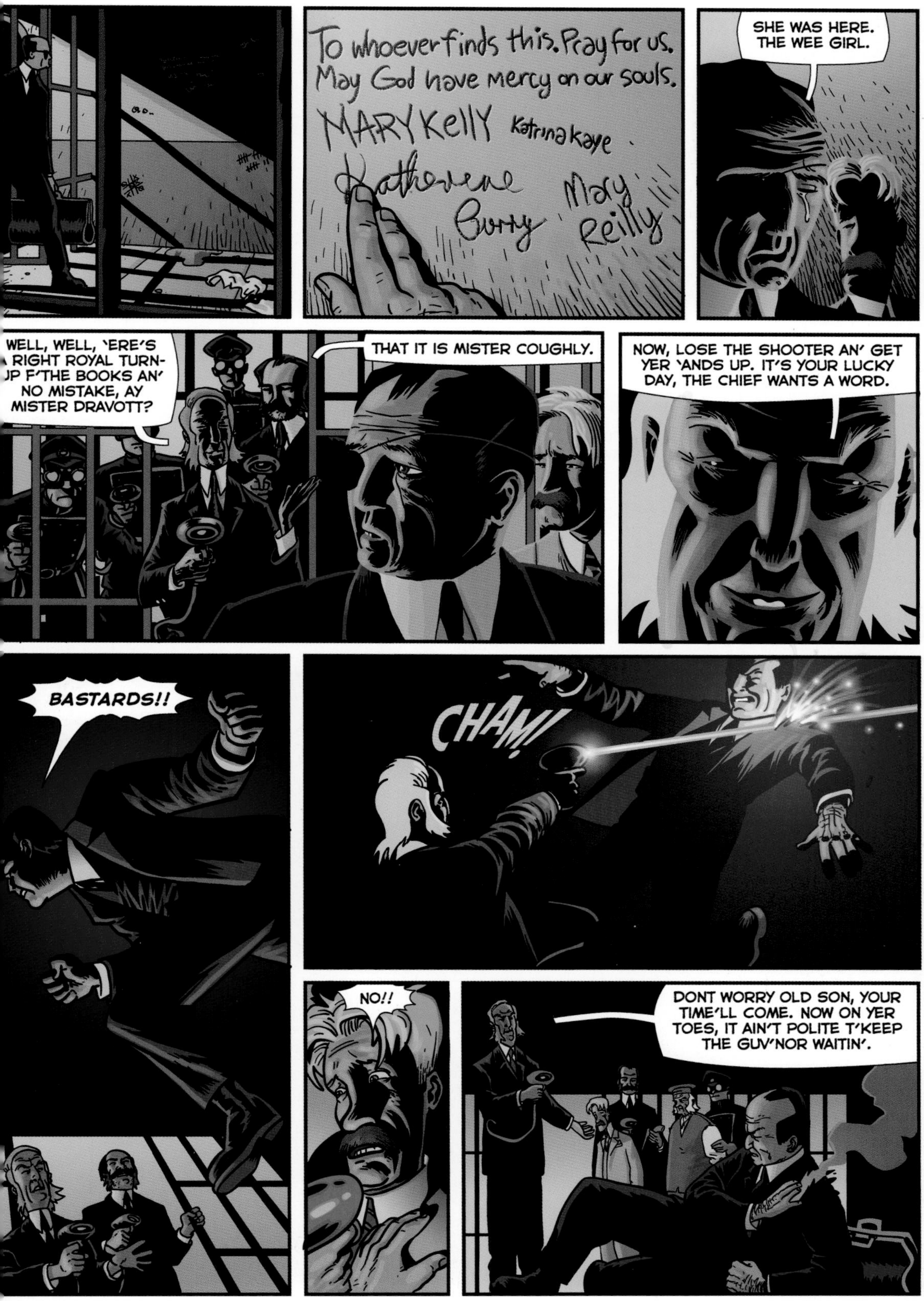
To whoever finds this. Pray for us.
May God have mercy on our souls.
MARY Kelly
Katrina kaye
Katherine Curry
Mary Reilly
SHE WAS HERE. THE WEE GIRL.
WELL, WELL, 'ERE'S A RIGHT ROYAL TURN-UP F'THE BOOKS AN' NO MISTAKE, AY MISTER DRAVOTT?
THAT IT IS MISTER COUGHLY.
NOW, LOSE THE SHOOTER AN' GET YER 'ANDS UP. IT'S YOUR LUCKY DAY, THE CHIEF WANTS A WORD.
BASTARDS!!
CHAM!
NO!!
DONT WORRY OLD SON, YOUR TIME'LL COME. NOW ON YER TOES, IT AIN'T POLITE T'KEEP THE GUV'NOR WAITIN'.

YOU!

ROBERT, MY DEAR FELLOW! THIS IS A SURPRISE. YOU'RE LOOKING REMARKABLY CHIPPER FOR A DEAD MAN I MUST SAY!

AND SERGEANT CURRIE, YOU APPEAR A TAD THE WORSE FOR WEAR. PLEASE, SIT DOWN BEFORE YOU FALL DOWN.

GET STUFFED!

AH, AS ELOQUENT AS EVER!

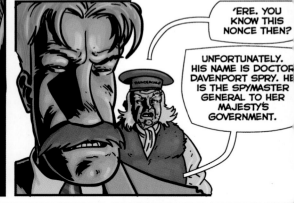

'ERE. YOU KNOW THIS NONCE THEN?

UNFORTUNATELY. HIS NAME IS DOCTOR DAVENPORT SPRY. HE IS THE SPYMASTER GENERAL TO HER MAJESTY'S GOVERNMENT.

I AM MERELY A CIVIL SERVANT AND PATRIOT.

YOU ARE A LIAR AND COWARD WITH NEITHER CONSCIENCE NOR MORALITY!

DO YOU EVEN REMEMBER THE NAMES OF THOSE MEN YOU LEFT TO DIE IN THE CRIMEA?

THOSE WHO PARTICIPATE IN THE GREAT GAME KNOW THE RULES. WE ARE ALL EXPENDABLE WHEN IT COMES TO THE DEFENCE OF THE REALM.

WHUT ABOUT TH' WEE GIRLS Y'TWO FACED BASTARD! WHUT CHOICE DID Y'GIVE THEM!

IS THAT WHAT THIS IS ABOUT? YOU'RE CHARGING AROUND LIKE A WHITE KNIGHT, SQUIRE AND KNAVE IN TOW, ALL ON ACCOUNT OF SOME GUTTERSNIPE SLATTERN!

HER NAME WAS KATHERINE CURRIE! SHE WAS MA NIECE AND NO MAN'S WHORE!!

OY, EASY!

AH, I SEE. MY CONDOLENCES SERGEANT. IF IT'S ANY CONSOLATION, SHE DIDN'T SUFFER.

SHE WAS A CASUALTY OF WAR.

WAR? WHAT WAR?

WHERE IS 'E THEN AY? WHERE'S TH'BLOODSUCKER Y'BIN FEEDIN' THEM POOR WENCHES TO?

PARDON?

FOR GOD'S SAKE NED, THERE IS NO DAMN VAMPIRE!

ACTUALLY, IN A MANNER OF SPEAKING THERE IS. WOULD YOU CARE TO SEE HIM?

I...YES ...YES!

TOO BLEEDIN' RIGHT!

YOU WEREN'T PRESENT DURING THE MARTIAN INVASION, WERE YOU ROBERT?

AS YOU WELL KNOW!

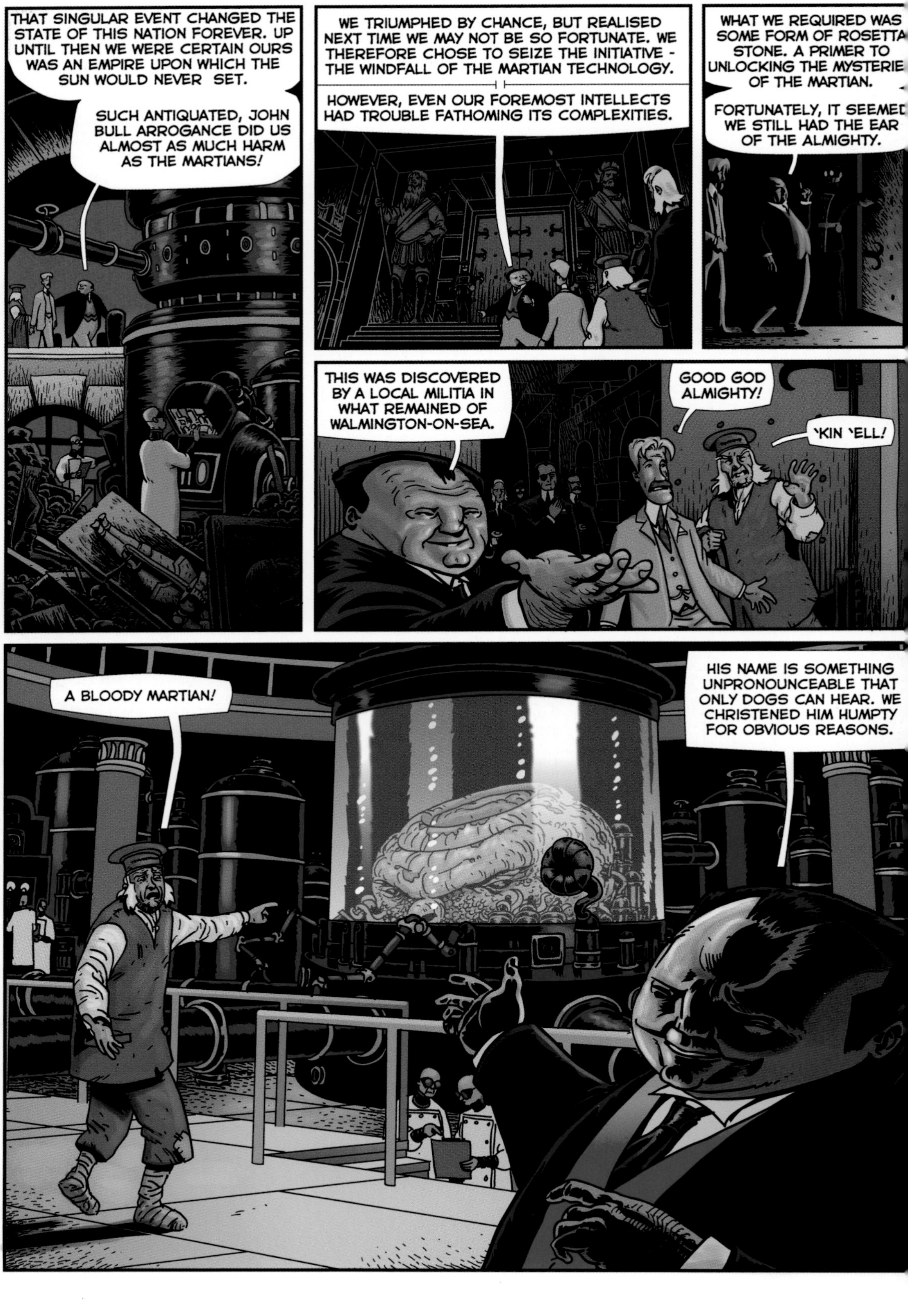
THAT SINGULAR EVENT CHANGED THE STATE OF THIS NATION FOREVER. UP UNTIL THEN WE WERE CERTAIN OURS WAS AN EMPIRE UPON WHICH THE SUN WOULD NEVER SET.
SUCH ANTIQUATED, JOHN BULL ARROGANCE DID US ALMOST AS MUCH HARM AS THE MARTIANS!
WE TRIUMPHED BY CHANCE, BUT REALISED NEXT TIME WE MAY NOT BE SO FORTUNATE. WE THEREFORE CHOSE TO SEIZE THE INITIATIVE - THE WINDFALL OF THE MARTIAN TECHNOLOGY.
HOWEVER, EVEN OUR FOREMOST INTELLECTS HAD TROUBLE FATHOMING ITS COMPLEXITIES.
WHAT WE REQUIRED WAS SOME FORM OF ROSETTA STONE. A PRIMER TO UNLOCKING THE MYSTERIE OF THE MARTIAN.
FORTUNATELY, IT SEEMED WE STILL HAD THE EAR OF THE ALMIGHTY.
THIS WAS DISCOVERED BY A LOCAL MILITIA IN WHAT REMAINED OF WALMINGTON-ON-SEA.
GOOD GOD ALMIGHTY!
'KIN 'ELL!
A BLOODY MARTIAN!
HIS NAME IS SOMETHING UNPRONOUNCEABLE THAT ONLY DOGS CAN HEAR. WE CHRISTENED HIM HUMPTY FOR OBVIOUS REASONS.

DOCTOOOR
DRYYYYY!!!

IT TALKS?

WE GAVE IT NO CHOICE. IT WAS LEARN OR DIE. A LINGUISTIC EQUIVALENT OF THE CARROT AND STICK.

OR A GUN T'THE HEAD.

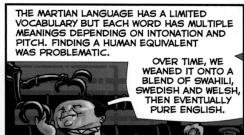

THE MARTIAN LANGUAGE HAS A LIMITED VOCABULARY BUT EACH WORD HAS MULTIPLE MEANINGS DEPENDING ON INTONATION AND PITCH. FINDING A HUMAN EQUIVALENT WAS PROBLEMATIC.

OVER TIME, WE WEANED IT ONTO A BLEND OF SWAHILI, SWEDISH AND WELSH, THEN EVENTUALLY PURE ENGLISH.

BLLLGGG HUUGGGG!

SOUNDS LIKE A LOON TAE ME!

A DECADE OF INCARCERATION AND INTERROGATION I'M AFRAID. HE SIMPLY BROKE. HE HAS THE MENTAL AGE OF AN INFANT NOW.

AND YOU COULDN'T PUT HUMPTY TOGETHER AGAIN?

NOT FOR WANT OF TRYING. HE'S OF THEIR ENGINEER CASTE, HE BUILT THE WAR MACHINES AND GRAVITY CANNONS THAT GOT THEM HERE.

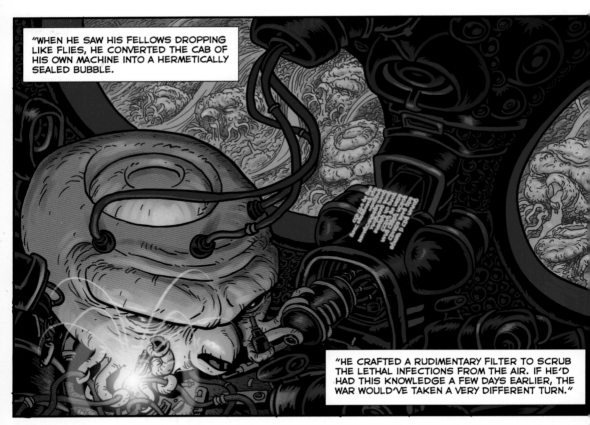

"WHEN HE SAW HIS FELLOWS DROPPING LIKE FLIES, HE CONVERTED THE CAB OF HIS OWN MACHINE INTO A HERMETICALLY SEALED BUBBLE.

"HE CRAFTED A RUDIMENTARY FILTER TO SCRUB THE LETHAL INFECTIONS FROM THE AIR. IF HE'D HAD THIS KNOWLEDGE A FEW DAYS EARLIER, THE WAR WOULD'VE TAKEN A VERY DIFFERENT TURN."

HIS EXPERTISE HAS PROVED INVALUABLE. THERE ISN'T A SINGLE MARTIAN DERIVED DEVICE IN USE, THAT DOESN'T OWE ITS ORIGIN TO THIS GHASTLY SQUAB.

OH, DEAR GOD. YOU FED THEM TO IT DIDN'T YOU? THE GIRLS.

I REMEMBER READING, DURING THE WAR, HOW THEY HERDED PEOPLE UP... LIKE CATTLE. BODIES WERE FOUND AFTERWARDS, DRAINED...BRITTLE...

...THEY DRANK THEIR BLOOD!

THEIR PHYSIOLOGY INDICATES THE THRIVE ON A DIET OF PURE PROTEIN IN ITS SIMPLEST FORM...BLOOD. WE TRIED FEEDING HIM ANIMAL BLOOD, HE ALMOST DIED.

WE NEEDED ANOTHER ALTERNATIVE BEFORE HE STARVED TO DEATH. HE WAS TOO VITAL TO LOSE!

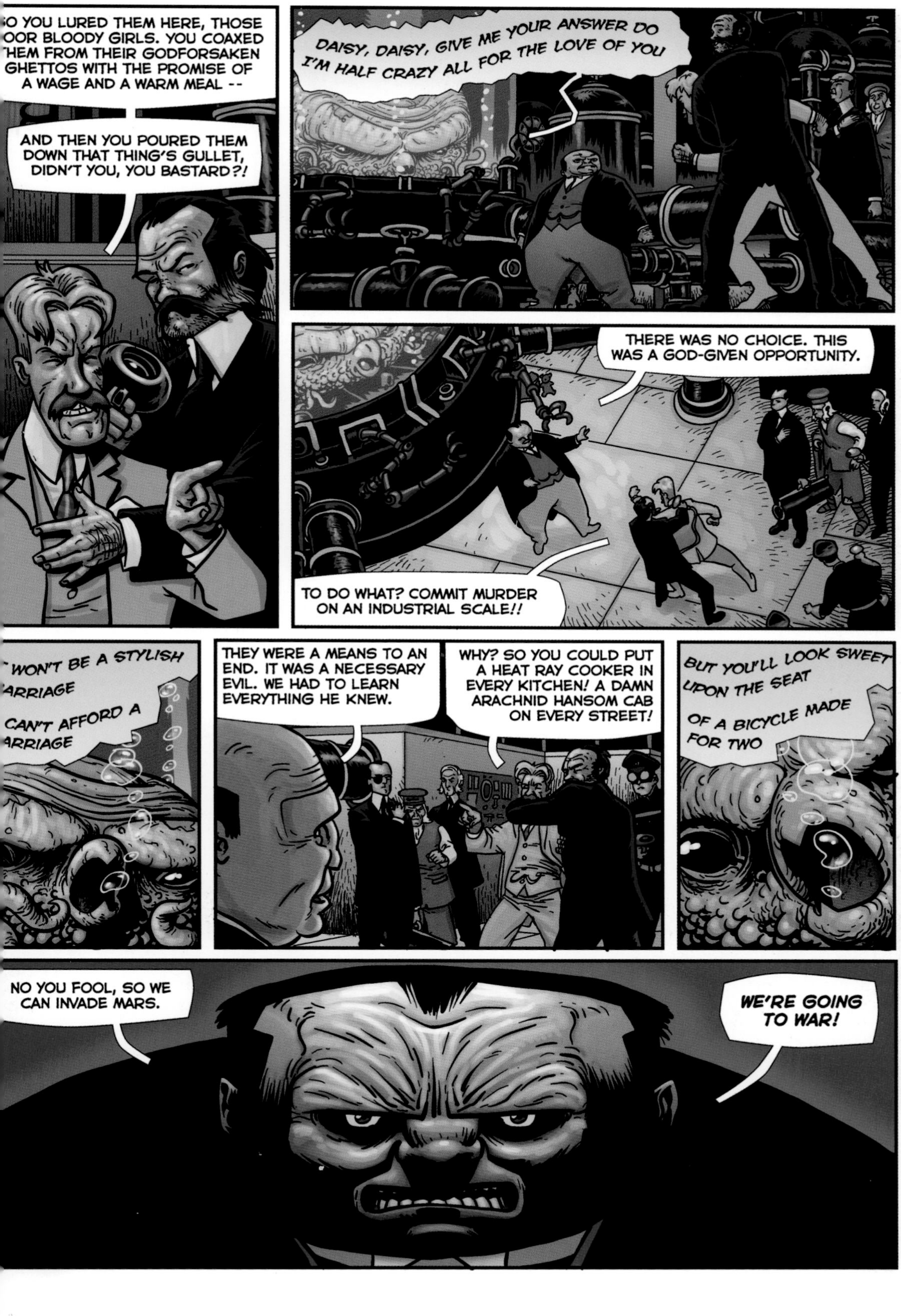
SO YOU LURED THEM HERE, THOSE POOR BLOODY GIRLS. YOU COAXED THEM FROM THEIR GODFORSAKEN GHETTOS WITH THE PROMISE OF A WAGE AND A WARM MEAL --
AND THEN YOU POURED THEM DOWN THAT THING'S GULLET, DIDN'T YOU, YOU BASTARD?!
DAISY, DAISY, GIVE ME YOUR ANSWER DO I'M HALF CRAZY ALL FOR THE LOVE OF YOU
THERE WAS NO CHOICE. THIS WAS A GOD-GIVEN OPPORTUNITY.
TO DO WHAT? COMMIT MURDER ON AN INDUSTRIAL SCALE!!
WON'T BE A STYLISH ARRIAGE
CAN'T AFFORD A ARRIAGE
THEY WERE A MEANS TO AN END. IT WAS A NECESSARY EVIL. WE HAD TO LEARN EVERYTHING HE KNEW.
WHY? SO YOU COULD PUT A HEAT RAY COOKER IN EVERY KITCHEN! A DAMN ARACHNID HANSOM CAB ON EVERY STREET!
BUT YOU'LL LOOK SWEET UPON THE SEAT
OF A BICYCLE MADE FOR TWO
NO YOU FOOL, SO WE CAN INVADE MARS.
WE'RE GOING TO WAR!

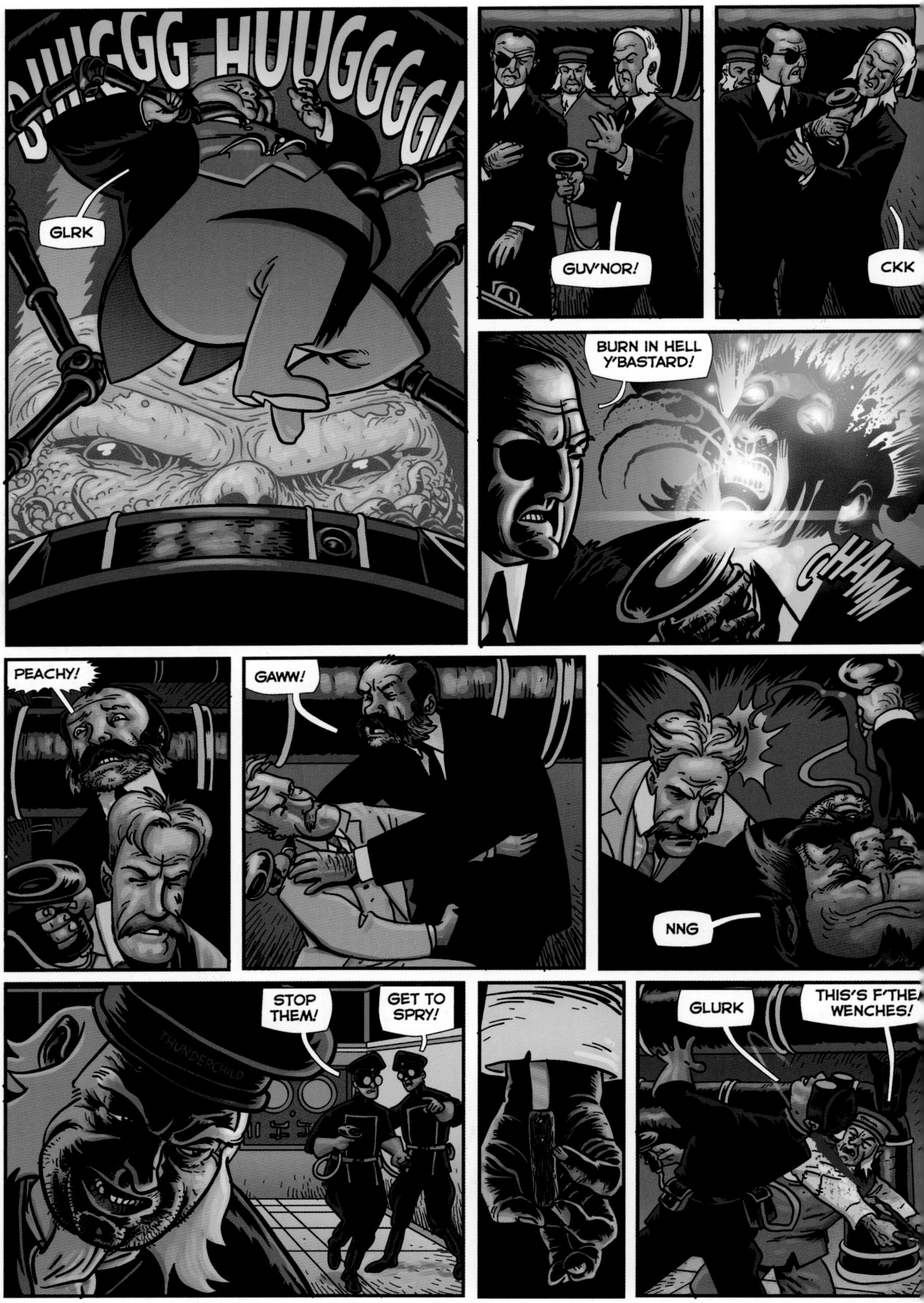
HUGGG HUUGGGG!
GLRK
GUV'NOR!
CKK
BURN IN HELL Y'BASTARD!
CHAWW
PEACHY!
GAWW!
NNG
THUNDERCHILD
STOP THEM!
GET TO SPRY!
GLURK
THIS'S F'THE WENCHES!

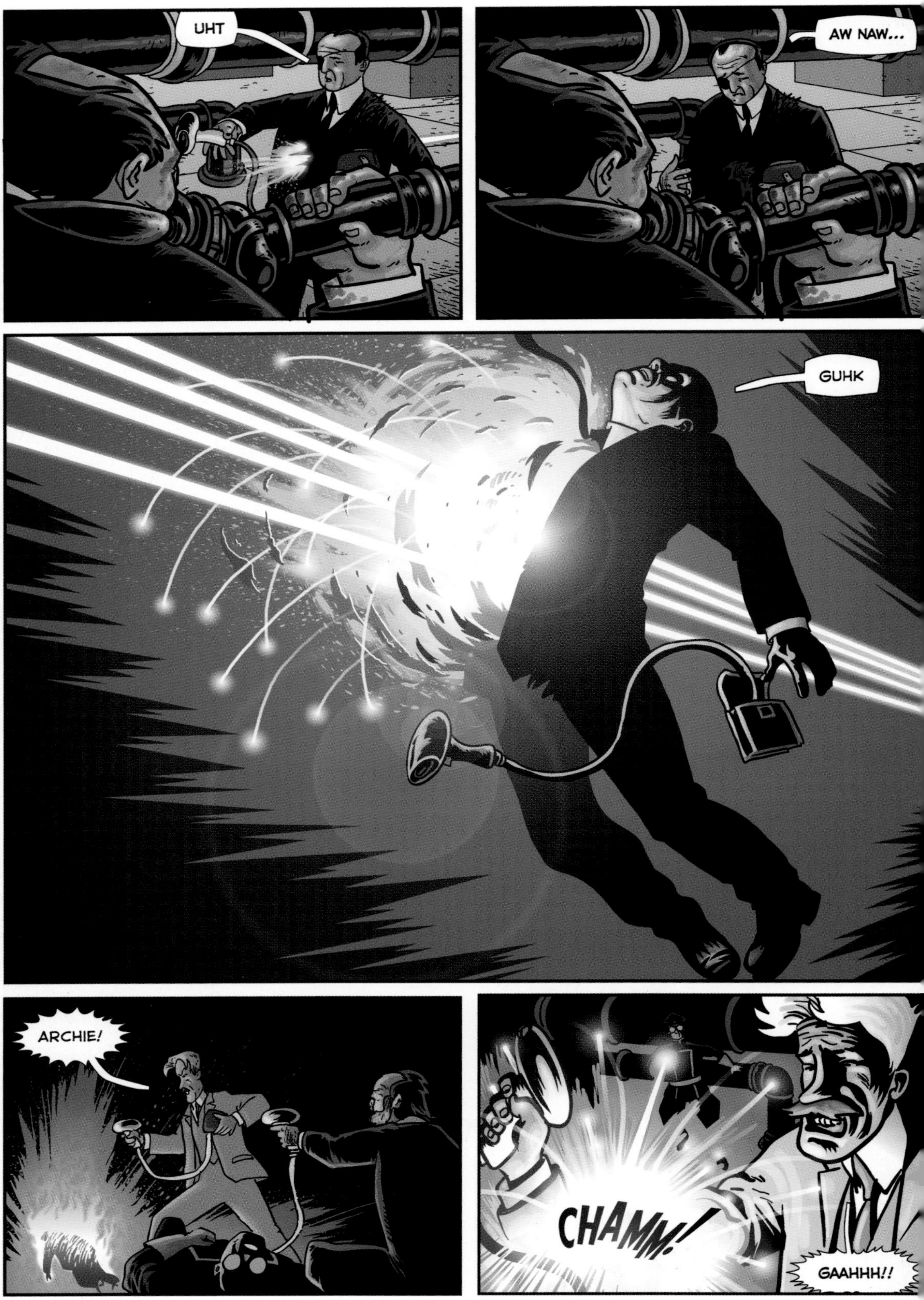
UHT
AW NAW...
GUHK
ARCHIE!
CHAMM!
GAAHHH!!

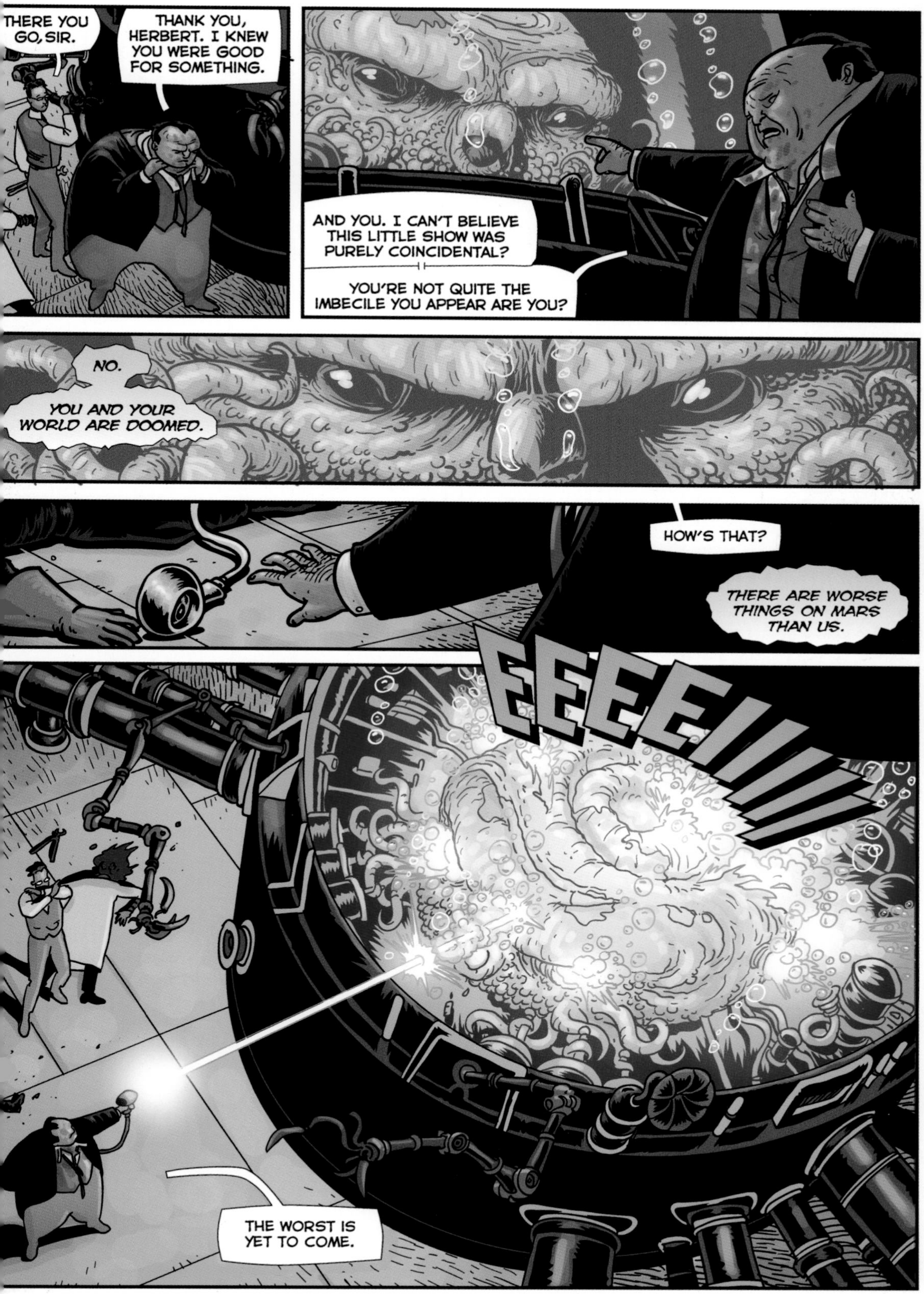
THERE YOU GO, SIR.
THANK YOU, HERBERT. I KNEW YOU WERE GOOD FOR SOMETHING.
AND YOU. I CAN'T BELIEVE THIS LITTLE SHOW WAS PURELY COINCIDENTAL?
YOU'RE NOT QUITE THE IMBECILE YOU APPEAR ARE YOU?
NO.
YOU AND YOUR WORLD ARE DOOMED.
HOW'S THAT?
THERE ARE WORSE THINGS ON MARS THAN US.
EEEE!!!!!
THE WORST IS YET TO COME.

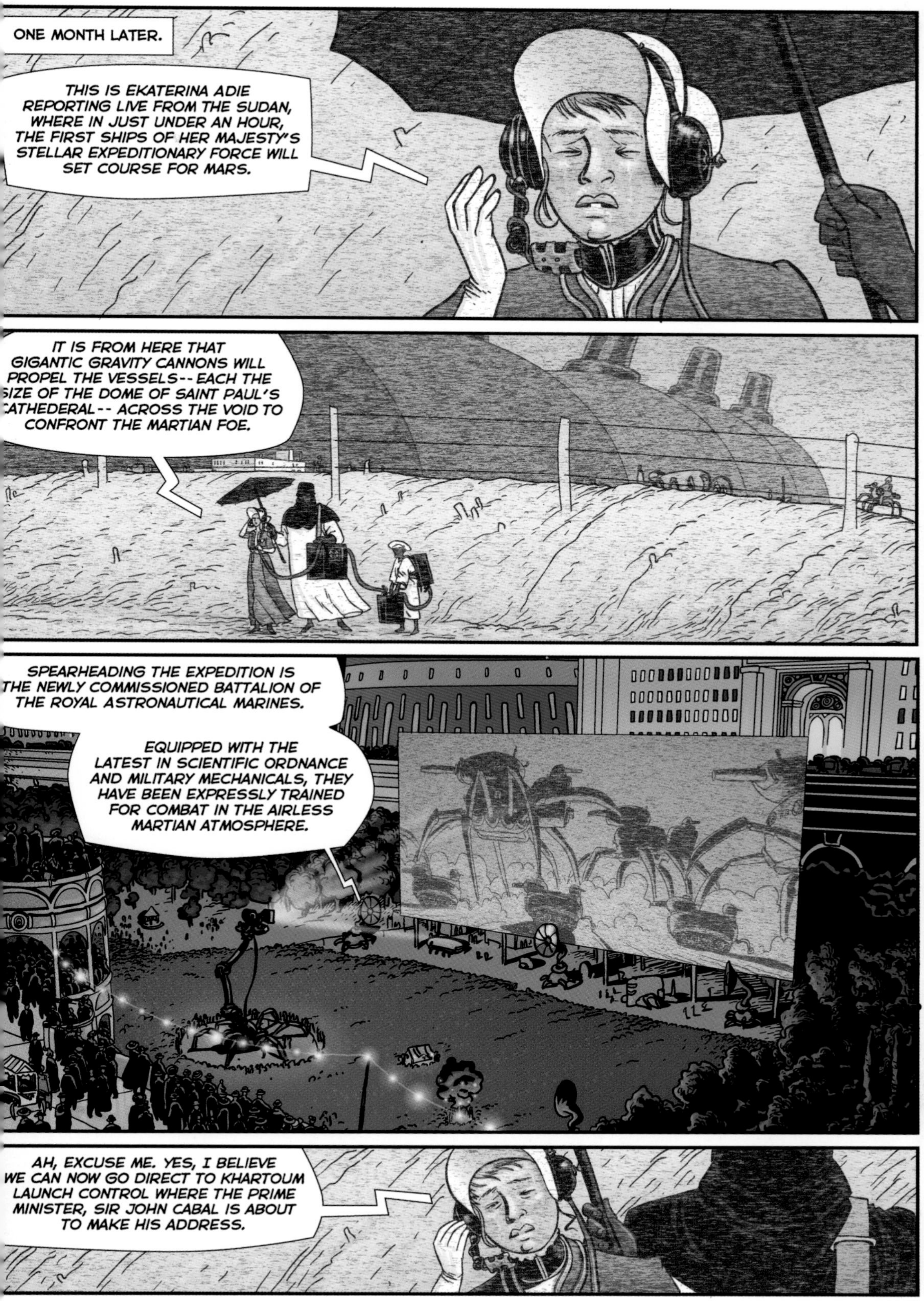
ONE MONTH LATER.
THIS IS EKATERINA ADIE REPORTING LIVE FROM THE SUDAN, WHERE IN JUST UNDER AN HOUR, THE FIRST SHIPS OF HER MAJESTY'S STELLAR EXPEDITIONARY FORCE WILL SET COURSE FOR MARS.
IT IS FROM HERE THAT GIGANTIC GRAVITY CANNONS WILL PROPEL THE VESSELS-- EACH THE SIZE OF THE DOME OF SAINT PAUL'S CATHEDERAL-- ACROSS THE VOID TO CONFRONT THE MARTIAN FOE.
SPEARHEADING THE EXPEDITION IS THE NEWLY COMMISSIONED BATTALION OF THE ROYAL ASTRONAUTICAL MARINES.
EQUIPPED WITH THE LATEST IN SCIENTIFIC ORDNANCE AND MILITARY MECHANICALS, THEY HAVE BEEN EXPRESSLY TRAINED FOR COMBAT IN THE AIRLESS MARTIAN ATMOSPHERE.
AH, EXCUSE ME. YES, I BELIEVE WE CAN NOW GO DIRECT TO KHARTOUM LAUNCH CONTROL WHERE THE PRIME MINISTER, SIR JOHN CABAL IS ABOUT TO MAKE HIS ADDRESS.

LADIES AND GENTLEMEN, WE ARE GATHERED HERE TODAY, TO BEAR WITNESS TO HISTORY IN THE MAKING. NOT OF STATE OR NATION BUT OF THE WORLD!

TEN YEARS AGO TO THIS DAY, THE MARTIAN RACE SET FOOT ON GOD'S OWN EARTH WITH THE OBJECTIVE OF SUBJUGATING HUMANITY BENEATH THE YOKE OF THEIR ALIEN TYRANNY.

THE BRIDGEHEAD OF THEIR VILE INTENT WAS THE VERY HEART OF THE CIVILISED WORLD, GREAT BRITAIN HERSELF. HOWEVER, WE HAVE REPULSED INVASIONS BEFORE, AS THE FRENCH AND SPANISH WILL ATTEST.

Live from Khartoum

AS ONE NATION WE RESISTED, SHOULDER-TO-SHOULDER. FROM OUR NOBLE MEN IN UNIFORM TO THE COMMON MAN IN THE STREET. WE STOOD FAST AND WITH THE AID OF THE ALMIGHTY WE PREVAILED.

NOW USING THE MARTIANS' OWN MACHINERIES AGAINST THEM, WE SHALL TAKE THE BATTLE BACK TO THEIR HOMES AND HEARTHS, WHERE WE WILL DELIVER SUCH A CRUSHING BLOW AS TO PREVENT THEM FROM EVER THREATENING OUR WORLD AGAIN!

BRITAIN ALONE BORE THE BRUNT OF THE CONFLICT WITHOUT THE SUPPORT OR SUCCOUR OF OUR NEIGHBOURS AND WE ASK NO ONE TO FIGHT OUR BATTLES FOR US NOW.

ON BEHALF OF MANKIND, WE WILL TAKE UP OUR SWORD ONCE MORE AND FORCE OUR FOE TO YIELD HIS WORLD TO US!

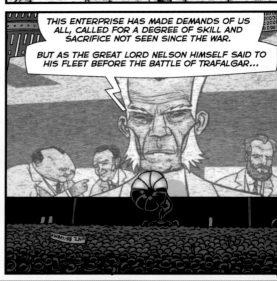

THIS ENTERPRISE HAS MADE DEMANDS OF US ALL, CALLED FOR A DEGREE OF SKILL AND SACRIFICE NOT SEEN SINCE THE WAR.

BUT AS THE GREAT LORD NELSON HIMSELF SAID TO HIS FLEET BEFORE THE BATTLE OF TRAFALGAR...

"ENGLAND EXPECTS EVERY MAN TO DO HIS DUTY." AND SO HE SHALL!

LYING BASTARD!!!

LIES! LIES! ALL LIES! THEY KILLED 'EM ALL, THOSE POOR BLOODY GIRLS! AND ARCHIE... DEAR ARCHIE... OH GOD!

70

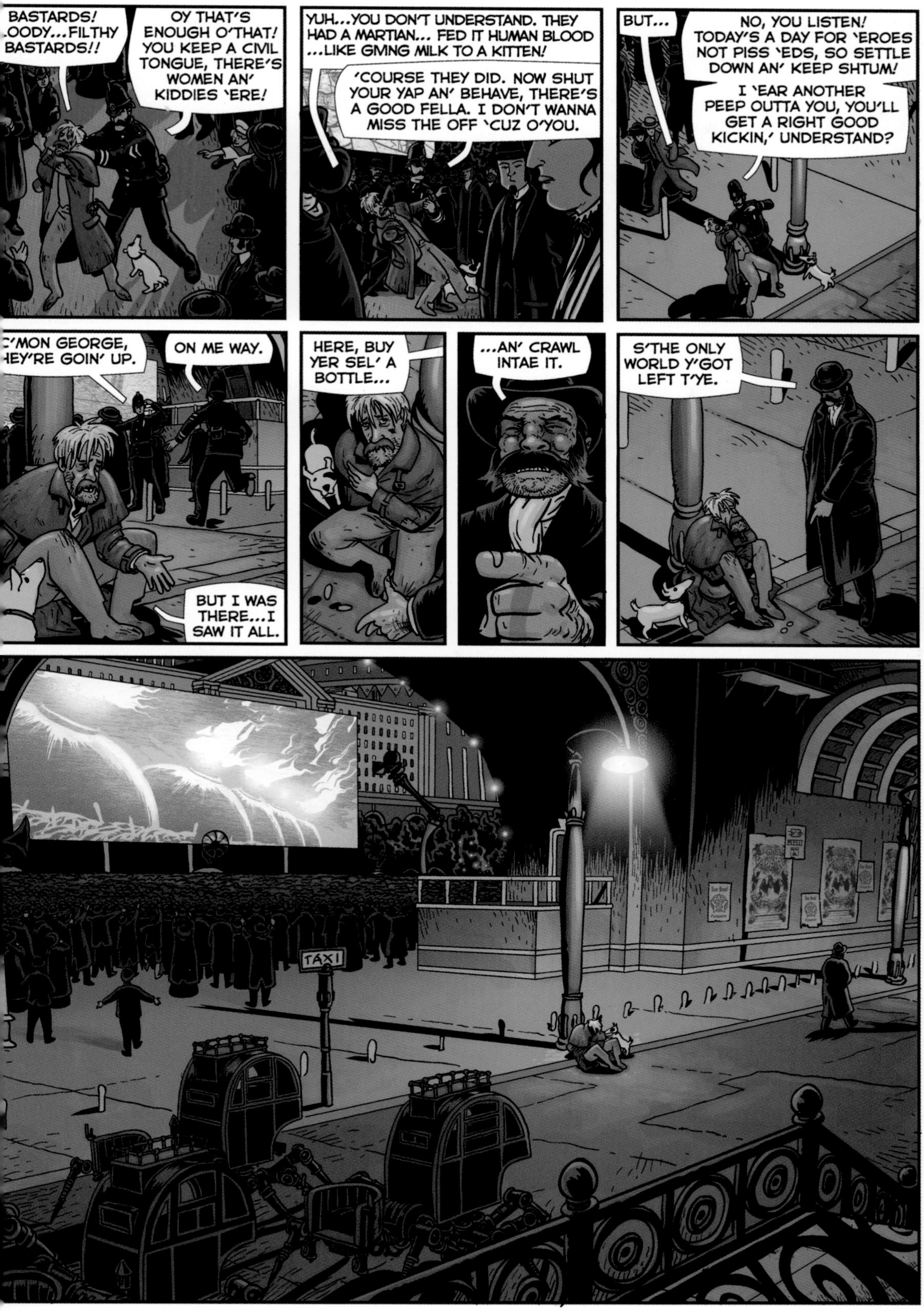
BASTARDS! LOODY...FILTHY BASTARDS!!
OY THAT'S ENOUGH O'THAT! YOU KEEP A CIVIL TONGUE, THERE'S WOMEN AN' KIDDIES 'ERE!
YUH...YOU DON'T UNDERSTAND. THEY HAD A MARTIAN... FED IT HUMAN BLOOD ...LIKE GIVING MILK TO A KITTEN!
'COURSE THEY DID. NOW SHUT YOUR YAP AN' BEHAVE, THERE'S A GOOD FELLA. I DON'T WANNA MISS THE OFF 'CUZ O'YOU.
BUT...
NO, YOU LISTEN! TODAY'S A DAY FOR 'EROES NOT PISS 'EDS, SO SETTLE DOWN AN' KEEP SHTUM!
I 'EAR ANOTHER PEEP OUTTA YOU, YOU'LL GET A RIGHT GOOD KICKIN,' UNDERSTAND?
C'MON GEORGE, HEY'RE GOIN' UP.
ON ME WAY.
BUT I WAS THERE...I SAW IT ALL.
HERE, BUY YER SEL' A BOTTLE...
...AN' CRAWL INTAE IT.
S'THE ONLY WORLD Y'GOT LEFT T'YE.
TAXI

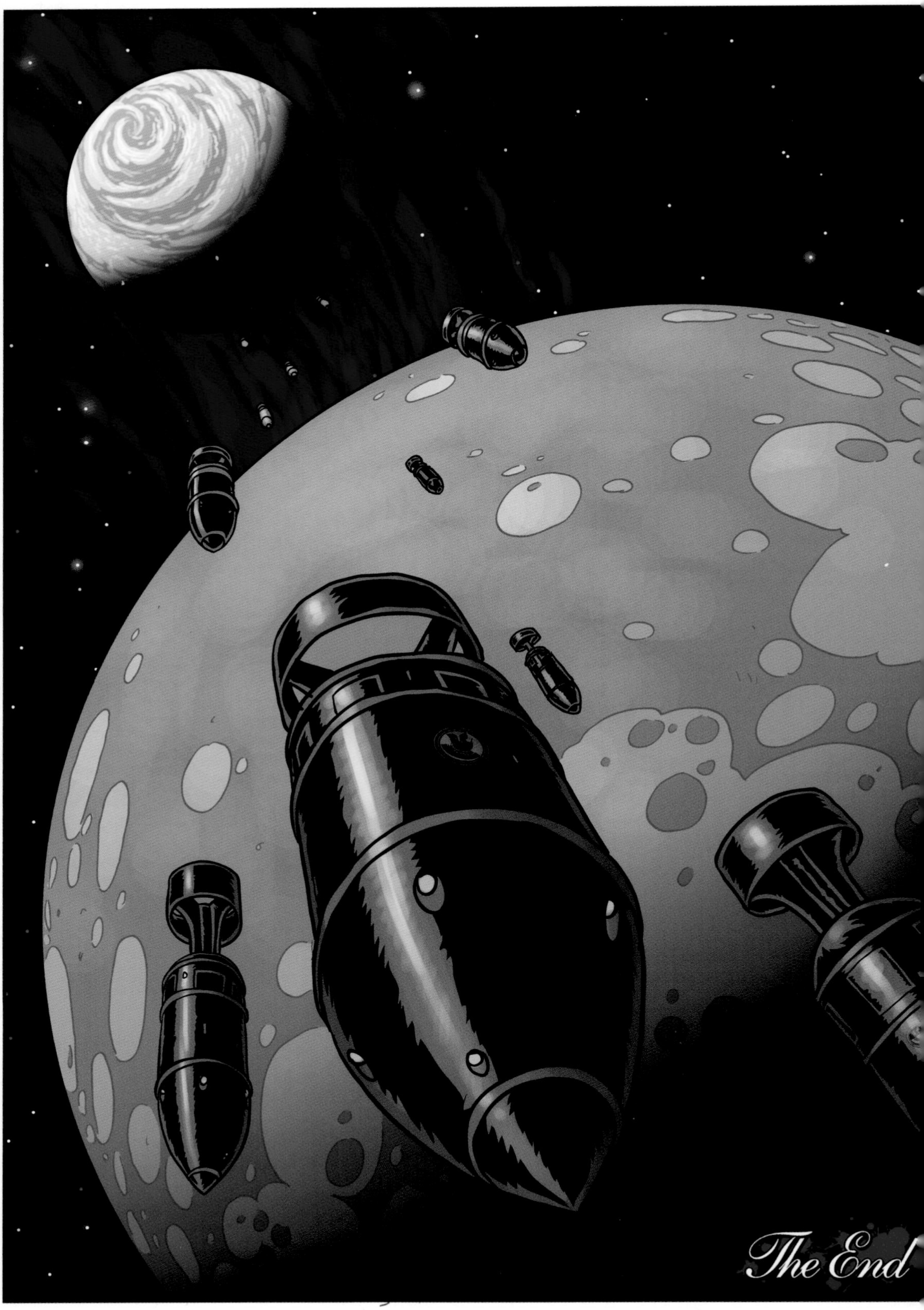
The End

Sketchbook and Deleted Scenes

all comments by D'Israeli

It's more than ten years since Ian Edginton and I first discussed the proposal which was to become *Scarlet Traces*. This first pen sketch is dated April 2nd, 1993.

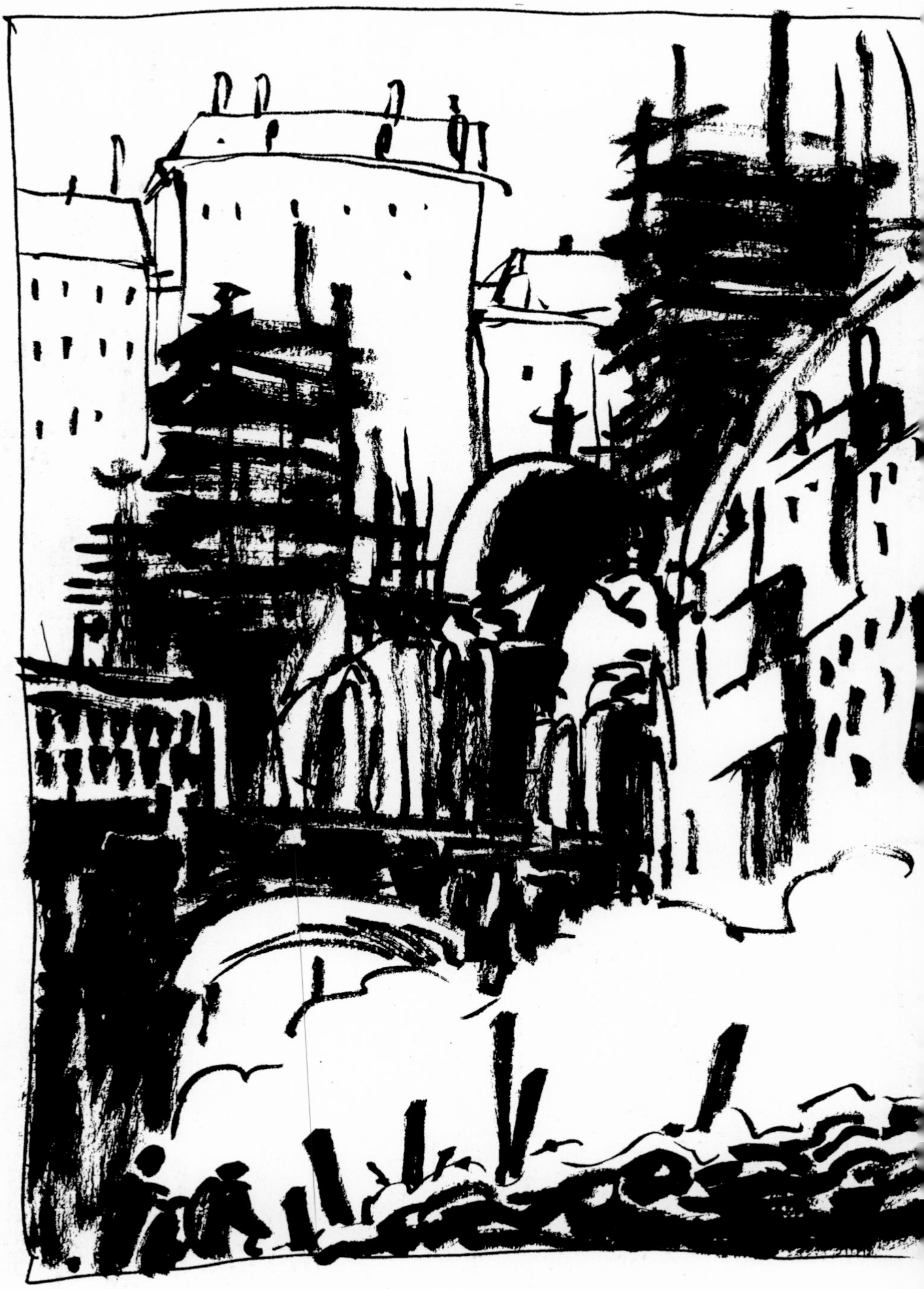

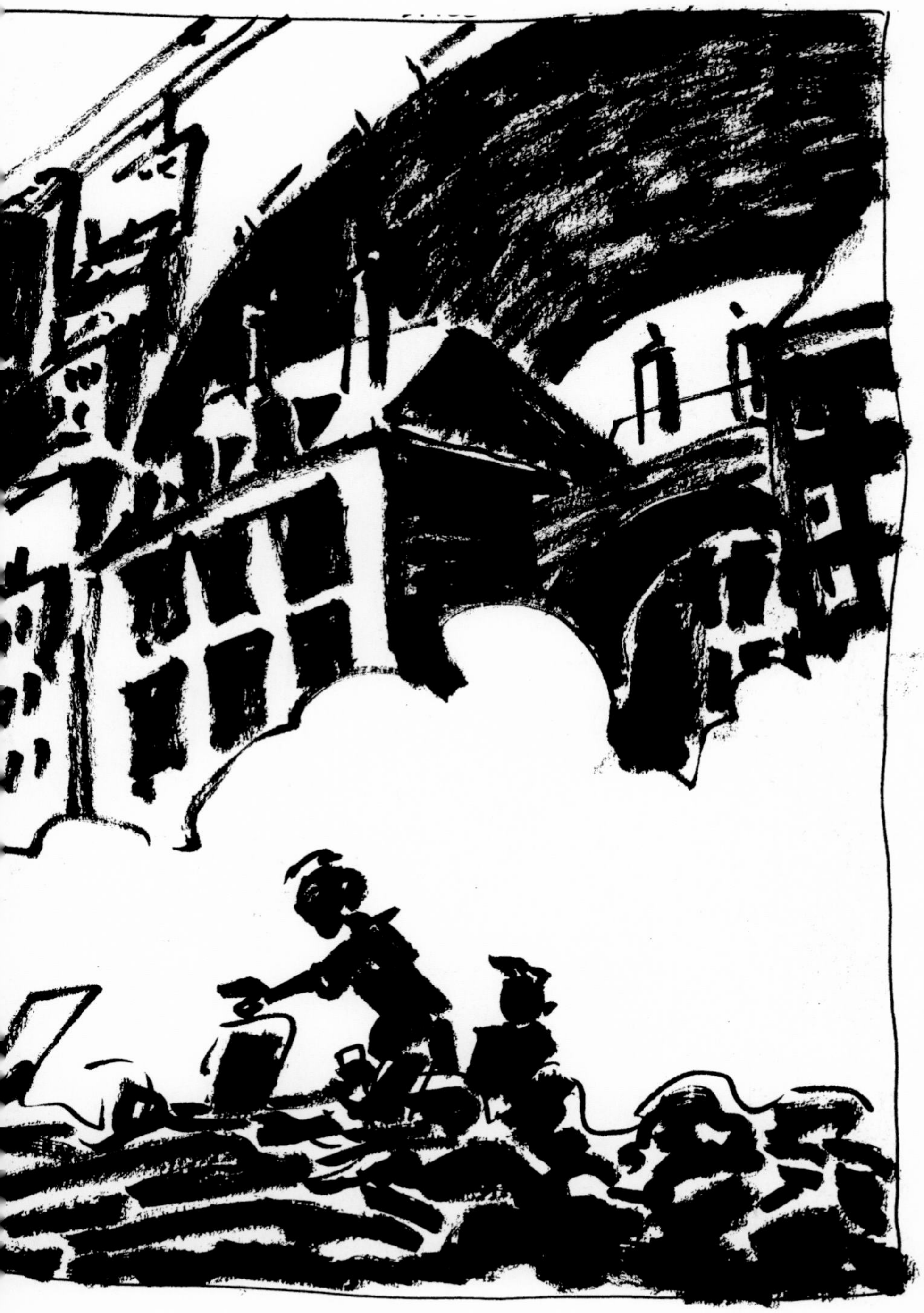

Although the Martians were long-defeated by the start of *Scarlet Traces*, we still needed a design for their Fighting Machines (right).

Scarlet Traces was originally commissioned by Coolbeans Productions Ltd. for use on the web, which meant we could include limited amounts of animation.

Coolbeans animators actually built a CGI tripod (below) for a proposed animated intro, which sadly was never made. They did get as far as making it walk, no mean feat for a three-legged device.

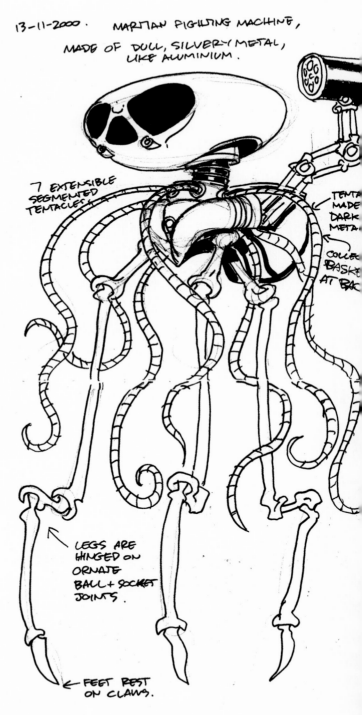

13-11-2000. MARTIAN FIGHTING MACHINE, MADE OF DULL, SILVERY METAL, LIKE ALUMINIUM.

7 EXTENSIBLE SEGMENTED TENTACLES

TENTA MADE DARK META

COLLE BASK AT BA

LEGS ARE HINGED ON ORNATE BALL + SOCKET JOINTS.

FEET REST ON CLAWS.

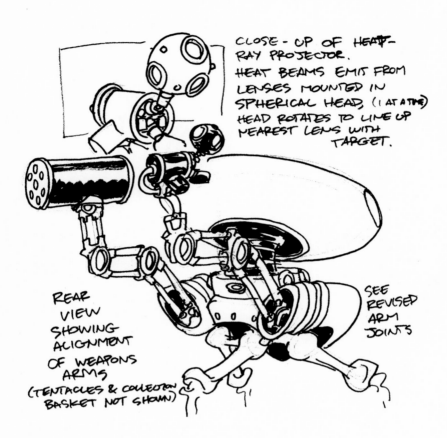

CLOSE - UP OF HEAT-RAY PROJECTOR.
HEAT BEAMS EMIT FROM LENSES MOUNTED IN SPHERICAL HEAD, (1 AT A TIME) HEAD ROTATES TO LINE UP NEAREST LENS WITH TARGET.

REAR VIEW SHOWING ALIGNMENT OF WEAPONS ARMS (TENTACLES & COLLECTION BASKET NOT SHOWN)

SEE REVISED ARM JOINTS

Because the Fighting Machine was to be built and animated, I had to draw it in detail from all angles, something I wouldn't need to do for a design appearing in an ordinary comic.

I also gave some thought to how the leg joints would work, and sketched out the rudiments of a walk cycle.

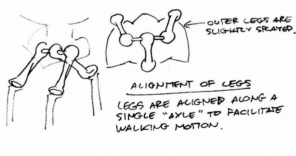

OUTER LEGS ARE SLIGHTLY SPLAYED.

ALIGNMENT OF LEGS

LEGS ARE ALIGNED ALONG A SINGLE "AXLE" TO FACILITATE WALKING MOTION.

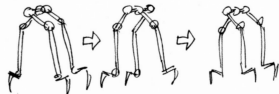

WALKING MOTION - TWO OUTER LEGS MOVE IN OPPOSITION TO INNER LEG. "ANKLE" JOINTS REVERSE

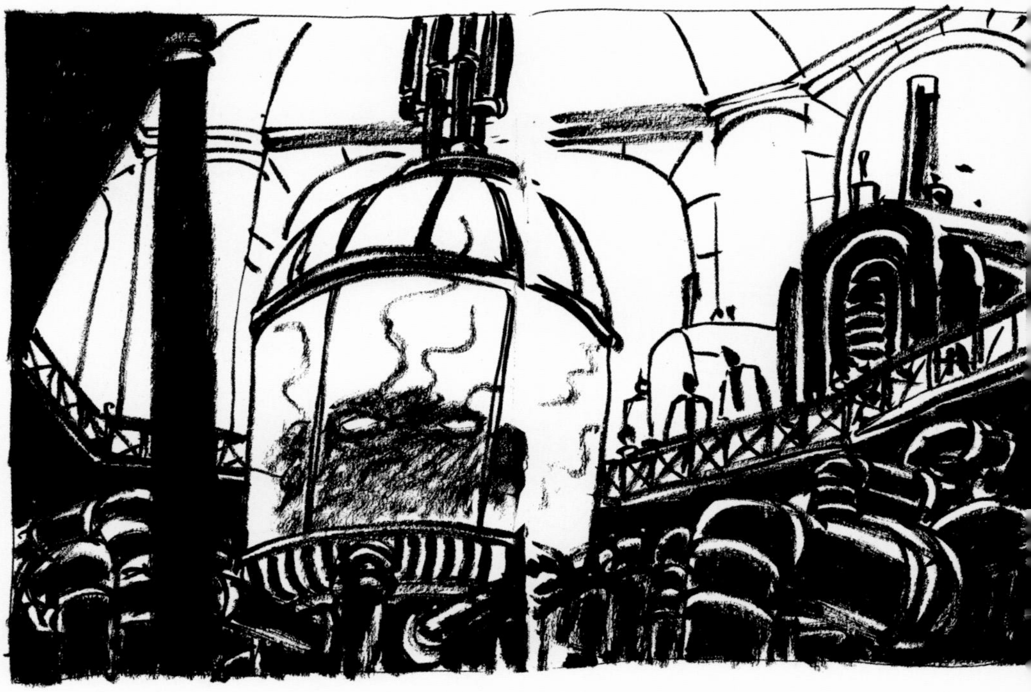

Above: the original sketch for the Martian tank room at Carfax Abbey. The basic layout was there from the start, though the room became a lot taller.

Below: the Martians, based closely on Wells' description.

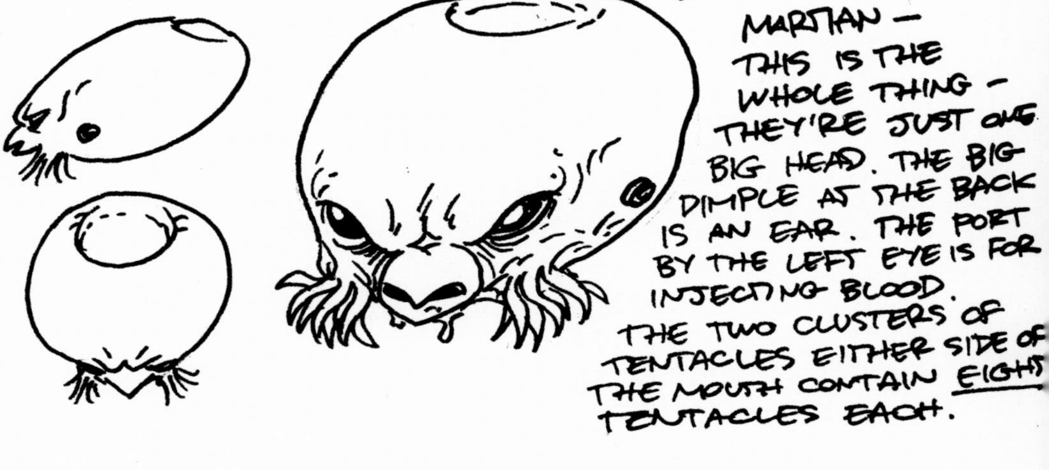

DARK, SLIMY, LEATHERY SKIN.
MARTIAN — THIS IS THE WHOLE THING — THEY'RE JUST ONE BIG HEAD. THE BIG DIMPLE AT THE BACK IS AN EAR. THE PORT BY THE LEFT EYE IS FOR INJECTING BLOOD. THE TWO CLUSTERS OF TENTACLES EITHER SIDE OF THE MOUTH CONTAIN EIGHT TENTACLES EACH.

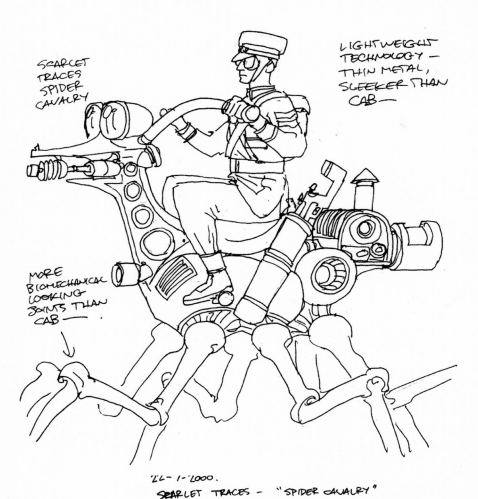

SCARLET
TRACES
SPIDER
CAVALRY

LIGHTWEIGHT
TECHNOLOGY —
THIN METAL,
SLEEKER THAN
CAB —

MORE
BIOMECHANICAL
LOOKING
JOINTS THAN
CAB —

22-1-2000.
SCARLET TRACES — "SPIDER CAVALRY"

A bove and right: whenever I collaborate with Ian Edginton, he always comes up with the best visual ideas. He was the one who suggested a Victorian world full of legged vehicles made with re-engineered Martian technology.

These are the first and final sketches for the "Spider Cavalry," the replacement for the Horse Guards.

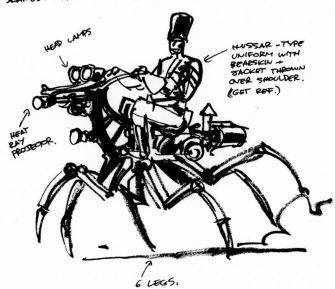

HEAD LAMPS

HUSSAR-TYPE
UNIFORM WITH
BEARSKIN +
JACKET THROWN
OVER SHOULDER.
(GET REF.)

HEAT
RAY
PRODUCER.

6 LEGS.

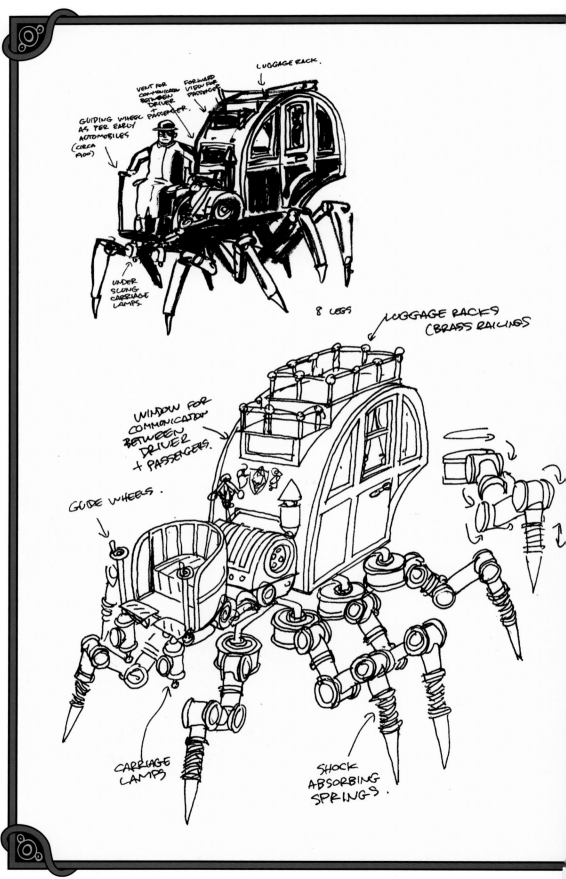

LUGGAGE RACK.

VENT FOR
COMMUNICATION
BETWEEN DRIVER
+ PASSENGER.

FORWARD
VIEW FOR
PASSENGER

GUIDING WHEEL
AS PER EARLY
AUTOMOBILES
(CIRCA
1900)

UNDER
SLUNG
CARRIAGE
LAMPS.

8 LEGS

LUGGAGE RACKS
(BRASS RAILINGS

WINDOW FOR
COMMUNICATION
BETWEEN
DRIVER
+ PASSENGERS.

GUIDE WHEELS.

CARRIAGE
LAMPS

SHOCK
ABSORBING
SPRINGS.

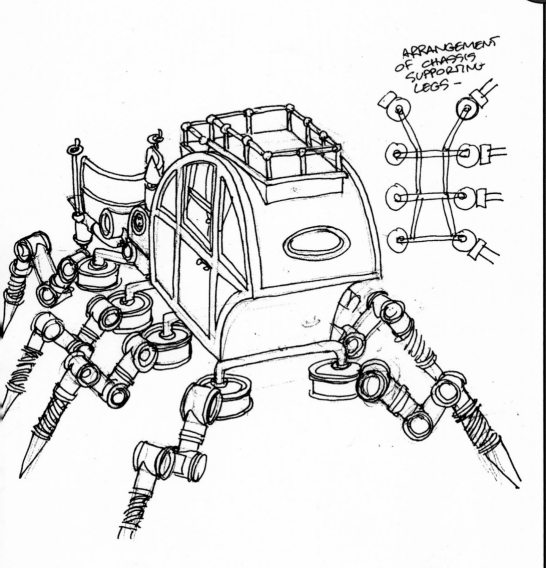

ARRANGEMENT OF CHASSIS SUPPORTING LEGS –

The *piece de resistance* of *Scarlet Traces* has to be the "Spider Cabs," again thought up by Ian. The basic idea is to have a Hansom cab mounted on eight mechanical legs. The driver's position and controls are based on the very earliest automobiles.

Though the Spider Cabs are a favourite of mine, they're a lot of work—if you're drawing a street full of traffic it adds up to an awful lot of legs. You'll notice that most of the busy street views in *Scarlet Traces* are seen from a distance, so I don't have to draw too many cabs in detail. I will also confess to cloning a single tiny cab lots of times in some shots!

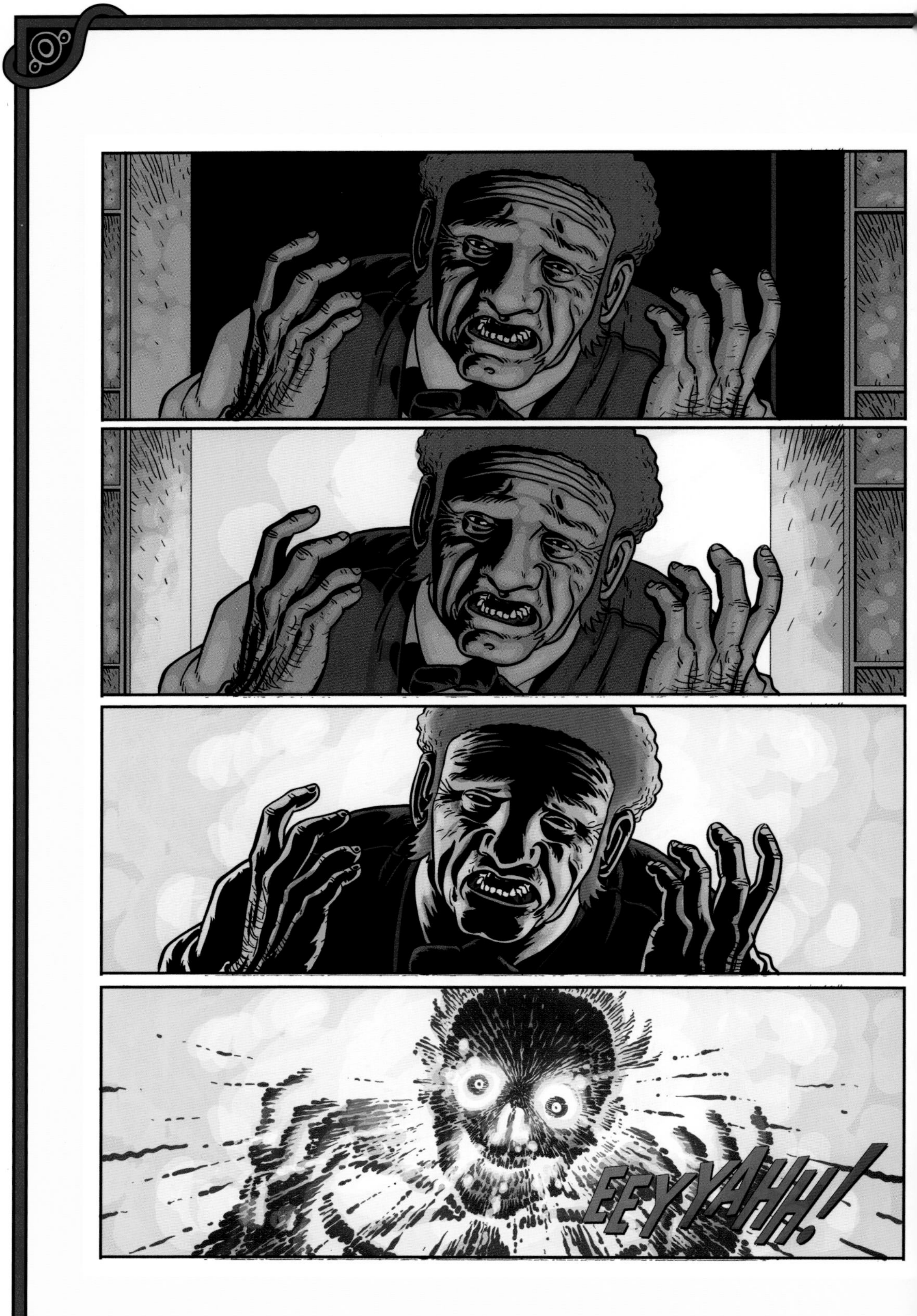
EEYYAHH!

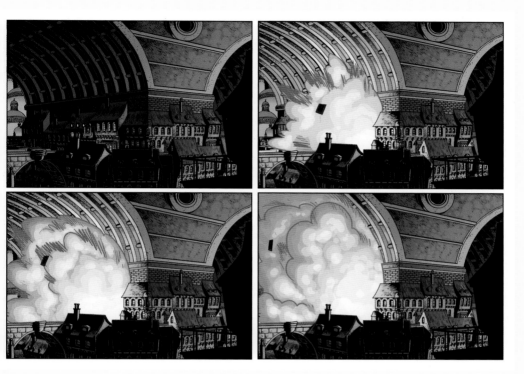

In *Scarlet Traces*' original web incarnation, most of the pages included limited animation effects. Many of these panels had to be altered or dropped, as we'd have had to include all the animated frames as separate comic panels to really make sense of them, and from a storytelling point of view they didn't warrant taking up that much space.

Left: the original, animated last panel of page 27 showing Sid the Landlord being blown up in gruesome detail. We substituted this with a wider shot showing Sid being blown off his feet as a fireball surges down the stairs from the pub.

Above: on the next page, 28, we kept the basic shot, but I re-painted the explosion to make it more dynamic. The original fireball had to be kept simple for animation purposes, the movement supplying the dynamism.

And yes, I did re-use the wide shot of the pub from page 26, but by the time I'd worked out how to overlay all the explosions and areas where the background is lit by the fireball, it didn't feel as if I'd saved much time!

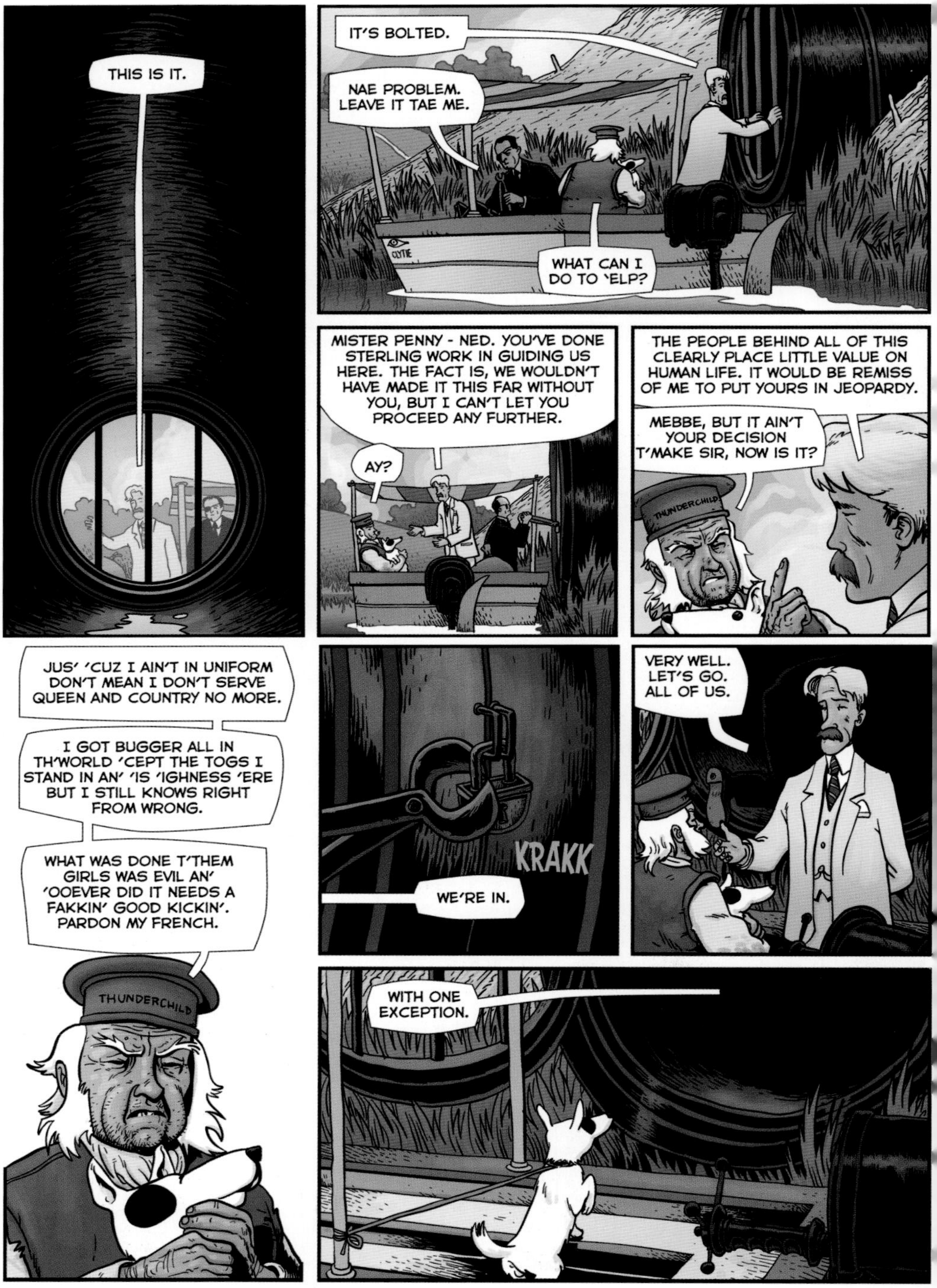
THIS IS IT.
IT'S BOLTED.
NAE PROBLEM. LEAVE IT TAE ME.
WHAT CAN I DO TO 'ELP?
MISTER PENNY - NED. YOU'VE DONE STERLING WORK IN GUIDING US HERE. THE FACT IS, WE WOULDN'T HAVE MADE IT THIS FAR WITHOUT YOU, BUT I CAN'T LET YOU PROCEED ANY FURTHER.
AY?
THE PEOPLE BEHIND ALL OF THIS CLEARLY PLACE LITTLE VALUE ON HUMAN LIFE. IT WOULD BE REMISS OF ME TO PUT YOURS IN JEOPARDY.
MEBBE, BUT IT AIN'T YOUR DECISION T'MAKE SIR, NOW IS IT?
THUNDERCHILD
JUS' 'CUZ I AIN'T IN UNIFORM DON'T MEAN I DON'T SERVE QUEEN AND COUNTRY NO MORE.
I GOT BUGGER ALL IN TH'WORLD 'CEPT THE TOGS I STAND IN AN' 'IS 'IGHNESS 'ERE BUT I STILL KNOWS RIGHT FROM WRONG.
WHAT WAS DONE T'THEM GIRLS WAS EVIL AN' 'OOEVER DID IT NEEDS A FAKKIN' GOOD KICKIN'. PARDON MY FRENCH.
THUNDERCHILD
KRAKK
WE'RE IN.
VERY WELL. LET'S GO. ALL OF US.
WITH ONE EXCEPTION.

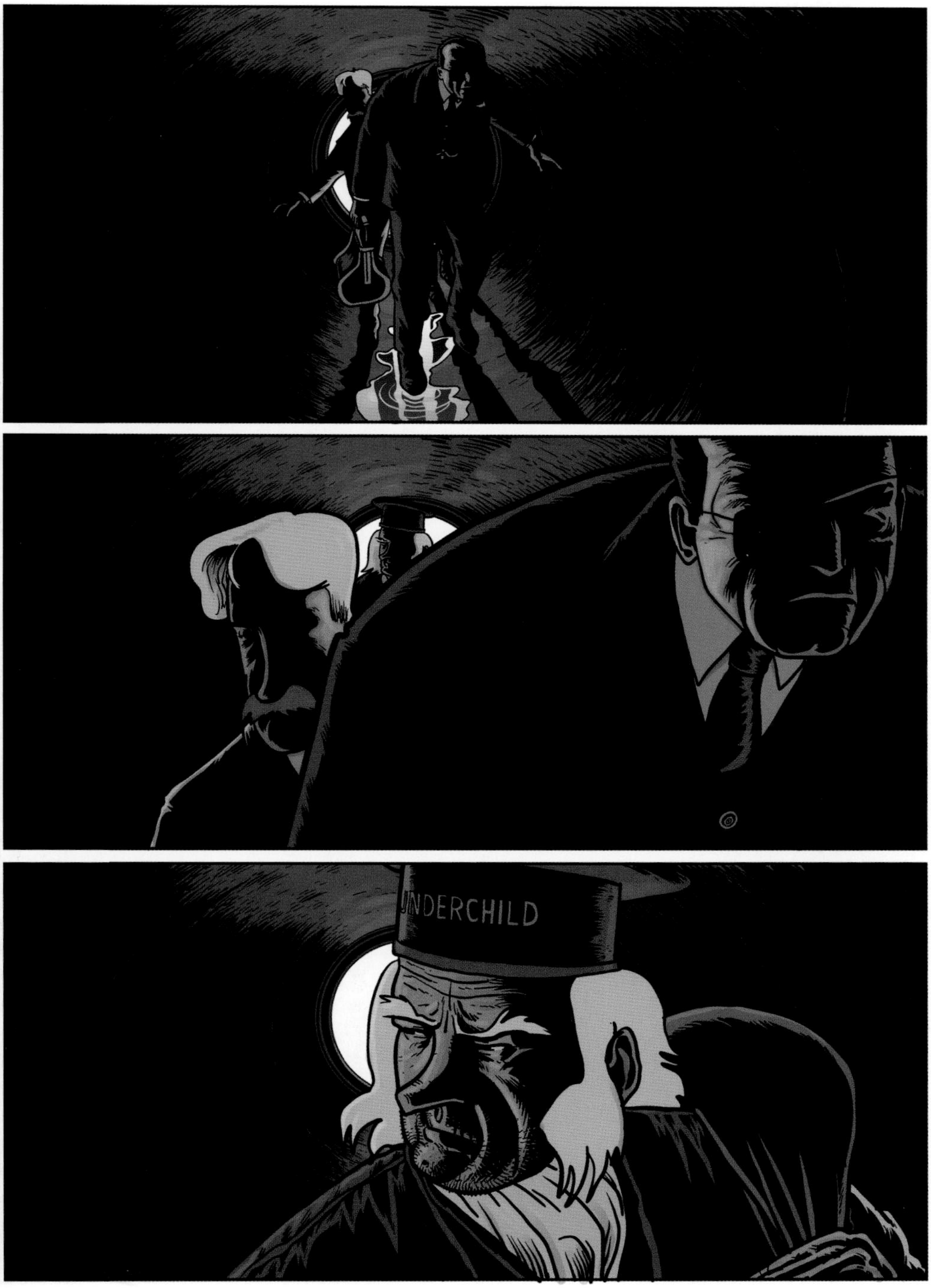
UNDERCHILD

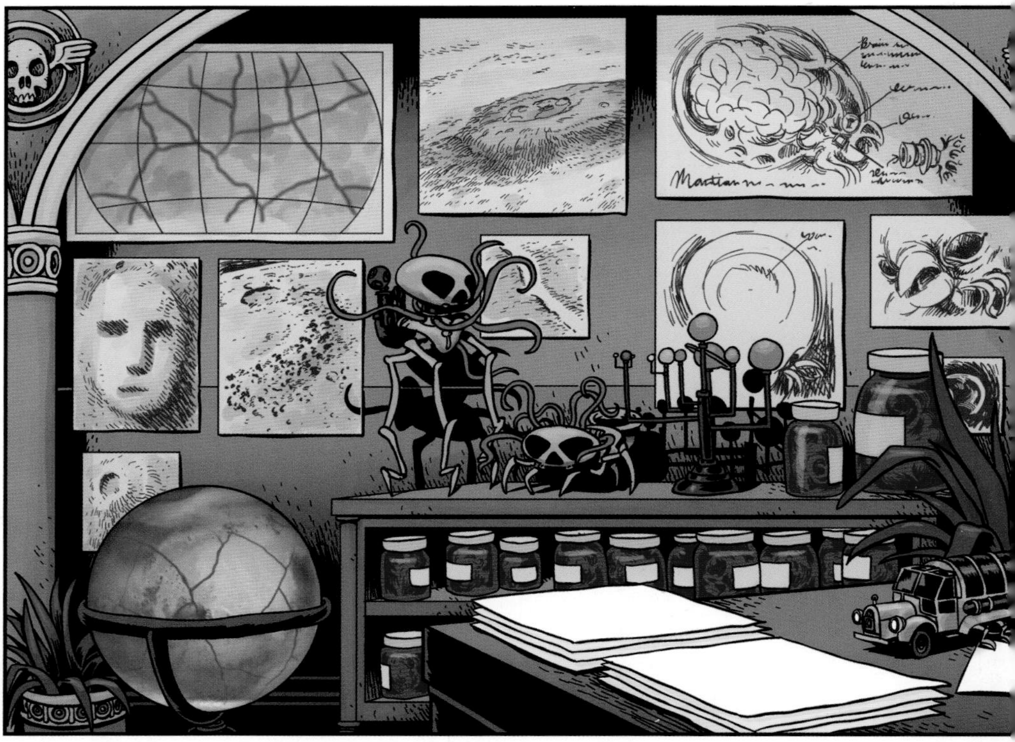

Above: a panning shot of Spry's office, complete with extracted Martian organs and model invasion vehicles. The clock on the far right would have been seen ticking down to Zero Hour, the launch of the invasion of Mars.

Previous pages: we regretted having to drop this original version of page 54 as it showed Ned's motivation for going into danger. The shot of Pikey straining at the lead is one of my favourite from the whole story. I think Pikey's fab, and that he should get his own series.

The display panels read:

Earth Time: 1904 July 23rd 11:23

Mars Time: 1904 July 3rd 12:10

Mission Time: Days:03 Hours:12 Minutes:00.16

IT'S TRUE, SURR... ALL THESE YEARS AN' YE NEVER SUSPECTED... AH'M A WUMMAN AN' AH LOVE YE!

GOOD LORD!

AND YET... IT MAKES SENSE OF THE STRANGE STIRRINGS I'VE ALWAYS FELT WHEN YOU WERE AROUND... THE FEELINGS I NEVER DARED ADMIT, EVEN TO MYSELF...

OH SERGEANT, THE YEARS WE'VE WASTED!

Left: a bizarre twist on Archie Currie's death scene, done as an April Fool's joke, though it only reached the pencil state. Note the blue pencil I use to rough out my drawing, and the perspective grids, which I use obsessively, even when it's only for a couple of lines on the floor, as here.

Following page: this originally went before page 21, and would have carried movie-style credits in the animated version.

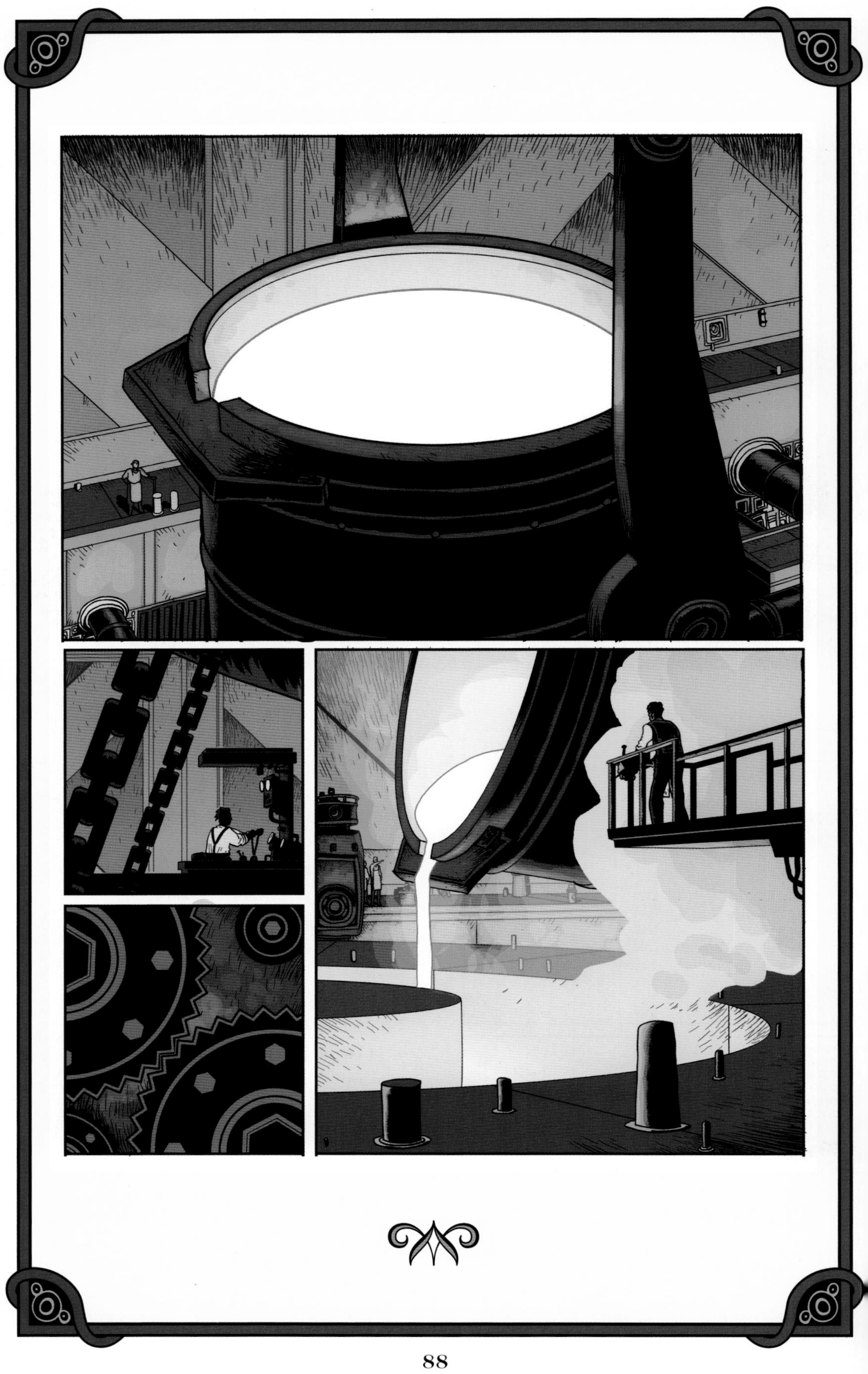